JEWELRY
MAKING

JEWELRY
MAKING

JO MOODY

CHARTWELL
BOOKS, INC.

A QUARTO BOOK

Published by Chartwell Books
A Division of Book Sales, Inc.
PO Box 7100
Edison, New Jersey 08818-7100

This edition produced for sale in the U.S.A., its
territories and dependencies only.

ISBN 0-7858-0634-2

This book was designed and produced by
Quarto Children's Books Ltd
The Fitzpatrick Building
188-194 York Way
London N7 9QP

Project Editor Simon Beecroft
Editor Kathryn Mellentin
Designer Nik Morley
Photographers Laura Wickenden and Colin Bowling
Indexer Hilary Bird

Creative Director Louise Jervis
Senior Art Editor Nigel Bradley

Many people helped with the creation of this book but the author would like to give special thanks to
Jackie Schou for her inspired designs and invaluable help with putting many of the projects together.

Manufactured by Bright Arts (Singapore) PTE Ltd, Singapore
Printed by Star Standard Industries (PTE) Ltd, Singapore

Contents

Getting started

Making your own jewelry is great fun, and not complicated or expensive to do. With just a little imagination, you can make wonderful works of art from almost anything – beads, buttons, scraps of fabric, and even yesterday's newspapers. This book is packed with projects that will suit both the beginner and the more experienced jewelry maker.

Materials

Lots of the projects in this book show you how to make your own beads using materials like salt dough, modeling clay, and even paper. You can also use bead substitutes, such as seeds, nuts, pasta, and shells to make fun jewelry.

The advantage of making beads is that you can decorate them in your own personal style. For this, you'll need poster or acrylic paints, and felt-tipped pens, plus a varnish to give them a shiny, hard-wearing finish.

Nylon or strong cotton line is essential for making your beads up into basic necklaces. Shirring elastic makes bracelets easy to get on and off, while leather thong makes simple pendants look stylish.

▲ *Totally unique designs can be created from unusual bits and pieces, such as buttons, pasta, unusually shaped beads, nuts, tool box bits, shells, and safety pins.*

Varnish

Adhesive

Leather thong

Paintbrush

Shoelace

Shirring elastic

Felt-tipped pens

Plastic line

Nylon line

Poster paints

String

"PROFESSIONAL" JEWELRY

To make earrings and brooches you will need to buy small metal "findings" – the bits used to put jewelry together. Simple necklaces and bracelets don't need findings but, for a professional finish, earring and brooch backs, clasp fastenings, jump rings, eye and head pins, calotte crimps, and bails are all essential. They are sold in craft stores or department stores.

The last material you will need is adhesive. PVA is usually suitable, but some projects require an "epoxy" adhesive.

A SHORT HISTORY

Jewelry has been worn since the beginning of time – to highlight a person's social status, to ward off evil spirits, or simply as a means of attracting attention. Prehistoric people wore the teeth or pelts (coats) of their prey. Ancient civilizations wore highly decorative headdresses and collars to display their power and wealth. Archaeologists have found ornate jewelry in the tombs of Egyptian pharaohs, along with wall paintings showing craftsmen working with beads and gold as long ago as 3,000BC.

Designs change constantly, influenced by fashion, the discovery of new materials, and new techniques. The history of jewelry is well worth investigating in your local library.

▲ *This ancient Egyptian necklace is more than 4,000 years old.*

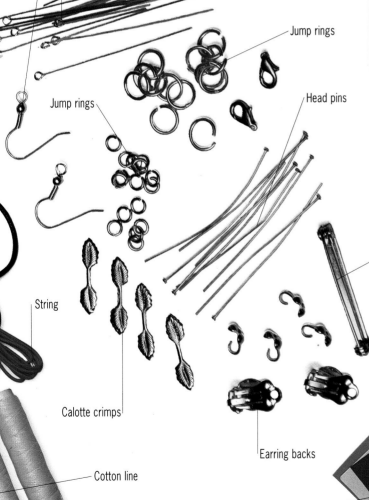

Eye pins
Earring hooks
Jump rings
Jump rings
Head pins
String
Calotte crimps
Brooch back
Earring backs
Cotton line
Scraps of fabric

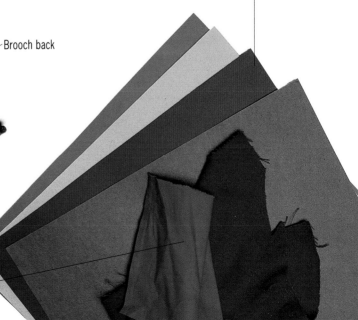

Colored paper

Tools, tips, and techniques

Most of the projects in this books are easy to make and need very little in the way of specialist tools and equipment. However, there are a few items you might find helpful. You will probably find most of them around the house, but, if not, they are easy to find and should cost very little. Here we show you the basic essentials.

A wooden board is useful for rolling out clay and dough. It is also useful for protecting surfaces when you are cutting, gluing, painting, or varnishing. Use an old chopping board or buy a piece of MDF, or blockboard, from your local DIY store.

For cutting out, you'll need scissors – ideally a pair of small-bladed scissors for intricate shaping, and a long-bladed pair for less fiddly jobs. A craft knife is also useful, but needs to be used under adult supervision.

Needles are used for threading beads together, and for sewing. For decorating your finished design, gluing, and varnishing you will need paintbrushes.

A compass is useful for piercing holes in hard materials, but should only be used under adult supervision. Pliers are also very useful. Here are some other tools you will need for the projects in this book.

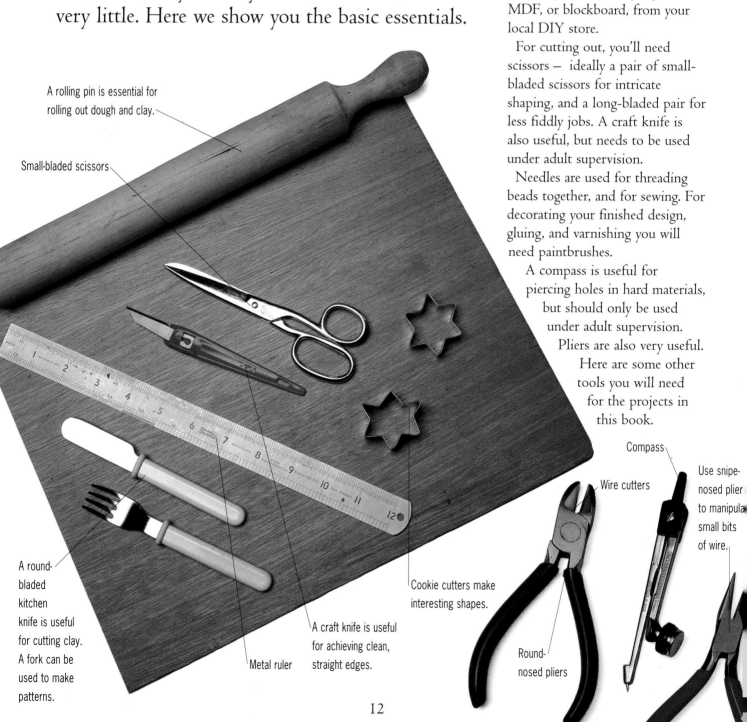

A rolling pin is essential for rolling out dough and clay.

Small-bladed scissors

A round-bladed kitchen knife is useful for cutting clay. A fork can be used to make patterns.

Metal ruler

A craft knife is useful for achieving clean, straight edges.

Cookie cutters make interesting shapes.

Compass

Wire cutters

Use snipe-nosed plier to manipula small bits of wire.

Round-nosed pliers

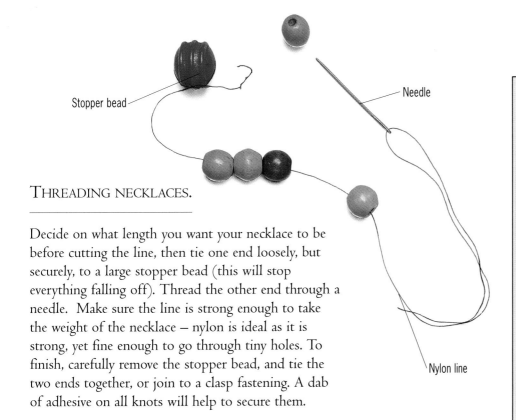

Stopper bead

Needle

Nylon line

THREADING NECKLACES.

Decide on what length you want your necklace to be before cutting the line, then tie one end loosely, but securely, to a large stopper bead (this will stop everything falling off). Thread the other end through a needle. Make sure the line is strong enough to take the weight of the necklace – nylon is ideal as it is strong, yet fine enough to go through tiny holes. To finish, carefully remove the stopper bead, and tie the two ends together, or join to a clasp fastening. A dab of adhesive on all knots will help to secure them.

DECORATING BEADS

Thread the beads, or bead substitutes, onto a knitting needle or wooden skewer,. Rest each end of the needle/skewer on a ball of Plasticine. This will keep the beads off the surface and make them easier to rotate whilst painting. Alternatively, you can use two pieces of styrofoam packaging to make a frame for the needle/skewer to rest in.

Leave beads to dry before threading.

KNOTTING

A simple overhand knot will be secure enough for most necklaces. Don't cut the ends too close to the knot – leave enough line to take each end back through the last few beads on either side. Secure with a dab of adhesive.

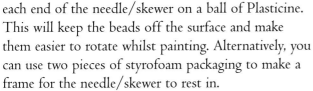

Rolled paper beads

R OLLED PAPER BEADS ARE VERY EASY TO MAKE. They are simply strips of paper tightly rolled around a knitting needle or wooden skewer. You can have lots of fun experimenting with color, pattern, size, and shape by using different kinds of paper, and by varying the length, width, and shape of the paper strips.

To make your beads last longer, spray them with varnish.

HAND PAINTED PAPER BEADS

You can make interesting beads from almost any kind of paper. Colorful wrapping paper, and pages torn from a glossy catalogue or magazine work well. Even pages torn from an old comic will do. But it's more fun to paint plain paper with your own design.

▼ Cut out wider triangles from magazine pages to make these long glossy beads. This design is created by cutting two lengths of shirring elastic, and weaving them in and out of the beads.

1 Paint your design. On the back, make pencil marks every inch along one edge, starting 1 inch in. Repeat along the opposite edge, but start 0.5 inches in.

2 Use a ruler to join the marks on the edges together to create elongated triangles, starting from the 0.5 inches mark. Cut out the triangles.

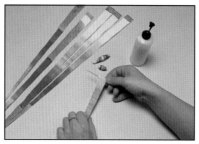

3 Starting at the widest end, roll each triangle around a knitting needle. Just before the end, dab adhesive on the wrong side, then finish rolling. Hold each bead until dry, then slide it off the needle.

4 Thread all the beads onto a length of nylon line using the method shown on page 13. Knot the two ends of the line together tightly, and tuck the loose ends in, to complete your necklace.

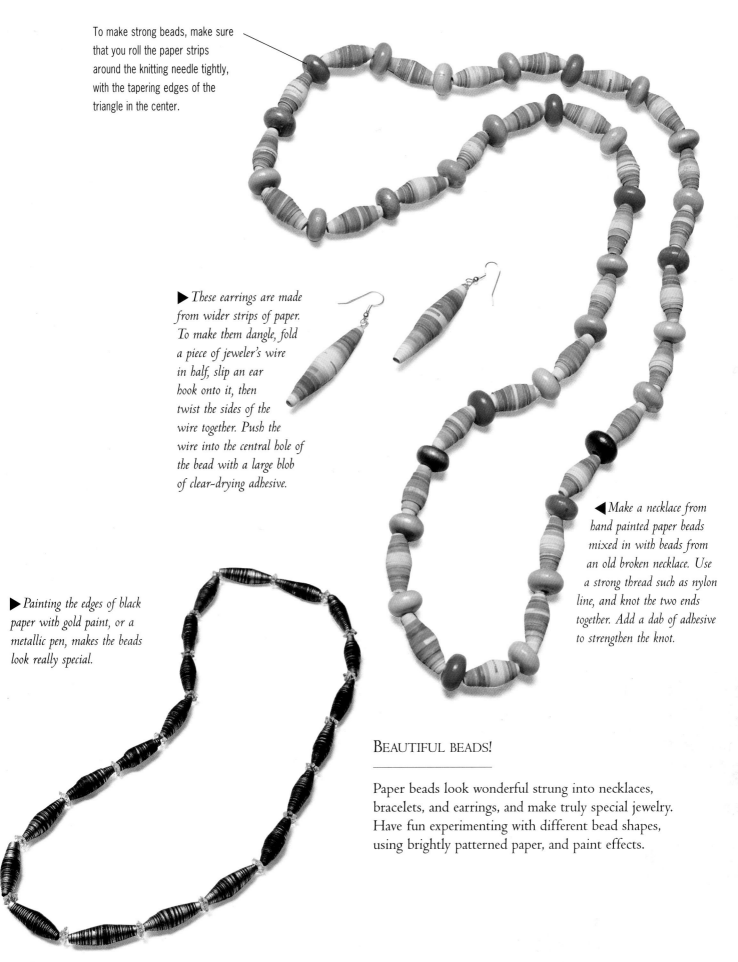

To make strong beads, make sure that you roll the paper strips around the knitting needle tightly, with the tapering edges of the triangle in the center.

▶ *These earrings are made from wider strips of paper. To make them dangle, fold a piece of jeweler's wire in half, slip an ear hook onto it, then twist the sides of the wire together. Push the wire into the central hole of the bead with a large blob of clear-drying adhesive.*

▶ *Painting the edges of black paper with gold paint, or a metallic pen, makes the beads look really special.*

◀ *Make a necklace from hand painted paper beads mixed in with beads from an old broken necklace. Use a strong thread such as nylon line, and knot the two ends together. Add a dab of adhesive to strengthen the knot.*

BEAUTIFUL BEADS!

Paper beads look wonderful strung into necklaces, bracelets, and earrings, and make truly special jewelry. Have fun experimenting with different bead shapes, using brightly patterned paper, and paint effects.

15

Magical Mosaics

CREATE WONDERFULLY INTRICATE MOSAIC designs by decorating cardboard with shiny paper shapes. For the most dramatic results, choose lots of different colors, and mix them all together. A quick look through a kaleidoscope will give you inspiration for shapes, and color combinations. With practice you can use other materials to create similar effects.

WHAT YOU NEED

Thick cardboard (mount board is ideal)

Pencil

Ruler

Craft knife

Paint

Paintbrush

Gummed shiny paper shapes

PVA adhesive

Varnish

Sharp thick needle or hammer and tack

Large jump ring

Pliers

Leather thong or cord

SQUARE PENDANT

Simple cardboard shapes can be transformed into spectacular pieces of jewelry by decorating them with shiny gummed paper shapes. Any strong cardboard will do, but special mount board, available from art stores, is ideal.

1 Draw a 1.5 inch square on the cardboard, and cut it out carefully, using a craft knife. Paint the square on both sides, and around the edges.

2 Stick the paper shapes all over one side of the square, to cover it. Leave the square to dry, then pierce a hole close to the edge in one corner.

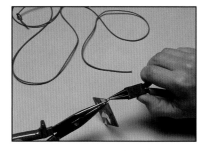

3 Using pliers, open up the jump ring sideways. Thread the jump ring through the hole, and use the pliers to close the ring again.

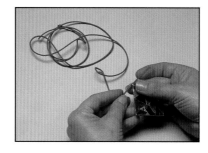

4 Make sure that both ends of the jump ring meet. Then thread the thong through the jump ring, and knot the ends together.

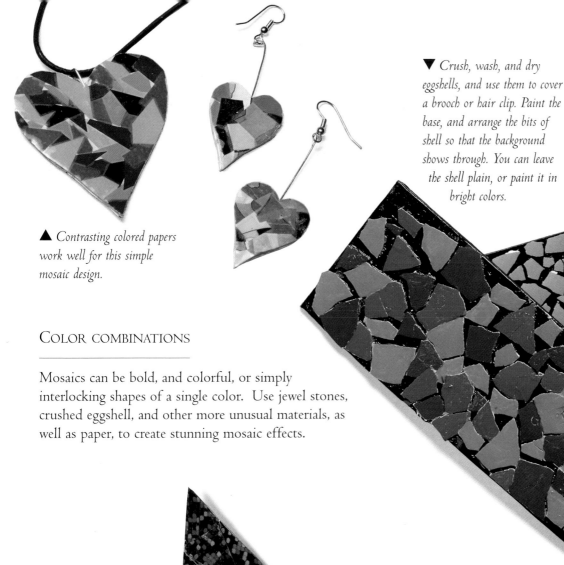

▲ *Contrasting colored papers work well for this simple mosaic design.*

▼ *Crush, wash, and dry eggshells, and use them to cover a brooch or hair clip. Paint the base, and arrange the bits of shell so that the background shows through. You can leave the shell plain, or paint it in bright colors.*

COLOR COMBINATIONS

Mosaics can be bold, and colorful, or simply interlocking shapes of a single color. Use jewel stones, crushed eggshell, and other more unusual materials, as well as paper, to create stunning mosaic effects.

▶ *Cut shapes from some colored wrapping paper, and glue them on to a kite-shaped piece of cardboard. Foil paper catches the light, and looks pretty, but experiment with other types of paper, too.*

◀ *Tiny flat-backed jewel stones in bright colors look dazzling glued on to cardboard circles.*

CAREFUL CUTTING!

Craft knives are very sharp. Always take great care when cutting. If you haven't used one before, ask an adult to help you.

▶ *A packet of tiny gummed moons have been used to decorate these triangle earrings.*

Hero worship

BY DECORATING A PLAIN CARDBOARD SHAPE with a picture of your favorite person, you can make unique jewelry that will be the envy of all your friends. Use a magazine cutting, or an old photograph of someone you love — from a pop star to a pet. Glue the image in place, and make up into a pendant, necklace, earrings, or even a charm bracelet.

Adhesive will help to keep the jump ring in place.

CHARM BRACELET

Cut out photographs of your favorite stars from a comic or magazine, and glue them on to small circles of stiff cardboard to make a fun charm bracelet. Jump rings, clasps, and lengths of chain can be bought from craft stores.

1 *Choose your images from old magazines or photographs. Place a coin over each of the chosen images, and draw around it carefully with a pencil. Cut out each of the circles.*

2 *Place the same coin on the cardboard, draw round it, and cut out a circle for each of your images. Paint one side of each circle a different color. Glue your images in place on the unpainted side of the "charm".*

3 *Pierce a hole close to the top edge of each charm. Open up the jump rings with the pliers, and insert one ring through the hole in each charm. Do not close up the jump rings at this stage.*

4 *Lay the charms along the length of the chain, spacing them evenly. Slip each open jump ring through a link on the chain. Close the rings carefully, so that the ends meet, or they will slip off the chain.*

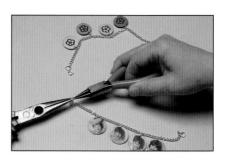

5 *Join a jump ring to one end of the chain. Join the last jump ring to the other end of the chain, slipping it through the loop on the bolt ring clasp at the same time. Draw a motif on the back of the charm.*

▲ *Cut out large motifs from colored wrapping paper, and stick on to cardboard. Cut around the shapes carefully, then cover them with self-adhesive plastic. Make into brooches by sticking a brooch finding, or a safety pin, to the wrong side.*

OUT OF THIS WORLD!

Here are some other ideas for "hero jewelry." If you use your imagination, the sky is the limit!

Instead of using self-adhesive plastic, you can protect your images by spraying them with varnish. If you take them to a local print shop, and laminate them, this will give them a very hard-wearing finish.

◀ *A stickpin is a fun idea, and can look great on a hat, coat, or jumper. These pins have rubber caps, and can be bought at specialist craft stores. If you can't buy a pin, use a safety pin instead, and keep it in place with a sticky label.*

◀ *Cut a star shape out of cardboard, and paint it a bright color. Glue a picture of your favorite hero or heroine to a circle of cardboard, and stick it in the center of the star. Use a length of chain or a leather thong to make the star into a spectacular pendant.*

More papier-mâche ideas

HERE ARE MORE WAYS TO USE THE LAYERED papier-mache technique. Pieces of card, with the ends joined together to make a circle, can be covered with strips of newsprint to create unusual bangles. Oblongs or squares of card, layered in the same way, can be made into hair slides and brooches.

▲ *This bracelet looks dramatic in black and gold. Use a metallic pen to draw your design on to four squares. Pierce holes in all the corners of each square, and thread with black shirring elastic.*

HAIR SLIDE

Make a jazzy hair slide by layering strips of old newsprint over a cardboard template. Ensure that the crown shape is completely covered — try to keep the points of the crown well defined.

WHAT YOU NEED

Pencil
A piece of corrugated cardboard
Marker pen
Scissors
Newsprint, torn into strips
PVA adhesive
Hair slide base (from craft stores)
Paint
Paintbrush
Varnish

MAKING A HAIR SLIDE

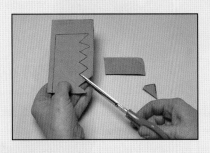

1 *Draw a crown shape on to corrugated cardboard. Draw over the outline in marker pen, and cut out carefully with scissors.*

2 *Paint the newsprint strips with adhesive, and cover the card shape with an even layer. Repeat once or twice, leaving to dry between each layer.*

3 *Open the hair slide, and place on the crown. Layer adhesive-covered newsprint over the hair slide base. Leave to dry. Repeat to secure.*

4 *Decorate with bright paints, then leave to dry. Finish with a coat of varnish, and leave to dry for 24 hours before using.*

▶ *Scrunch up a length of paper, and bring the ends together, to make a circle. Use sticky tape to hold the ends together. Layer with pasted paper until rigid, then decorate with a bold design.*

Finish with a coat of varnish.

◀ *To make different shaped bangles, make a base from strips of card stuck together with sticky tape.*

PILES OF PAPER

Use the layered paper technique to make all kinds of interesting jewelry. Cut out different shaped templates, or join cardboard together with sticky tape to make circles for a bangle.

▼ *Paint your hair slide in bold colors. This design is easy to copy, but you can have lots of fun designing your own.*

▲ *Use strips of wrapping paper to give a new look to a hair band, and bangle. You only need one layer of paper, just to cover the surface, and a couple of coats of varnish to protect it.*

Pressed paper pulp

This papier-mache technique uses paper pulp made from tissue paper or newsprint. The paper is soaked in water until soft, then mashed with a fork, or – if allowed – with an electric blender. The pulp is then squeezed until almost dry, and shaped into beads, pressed into cookie cutters, or molded on to card templates, which when decorated can be used for earrings, brooches, or pendants.

▲ *Cut out the bird shape from cardboard, and add a little pulp to give texture. Paint in bright colors, then add the detail in black, or another contrasting paint.*

Chunky necklace

Paper pulp is a lot of fun to work with. This chunky necklace is an easy design to start with, but once you get going you will soon want to move on to more complicated pulping ideas.

What you need

Sheets of tissue paper or newsprint

Scissors

Bowl

Fork or electric blender

A tablespoon of made up wallpaper paste

Sieve

Cocktail sticks or wooden skewers

White poster paint

Colored paints

Plasticine

Varnish

Nylon line

1 *Cut the tissue paper, or newsprint, into tiny pieces, place in a bowl, and cover with warm water. Leave to soak for several hours until soft, then mash.*

2 *Strain the mixture through a sieve, lightly squeezing out the water. Return to the bowl, and mix with a tablespoon of wallpaper paste. Strain again.*

3 *Mold the pulp into beads shapes, and leave to dry somewhere warm. Putting them on a cake rack will speed up the drying time. When almost dry, pierce with a cocktail stick.*

4 *Paint the beads with white poster paint first, then, when, dry in the colors of your choice. Finish with a coat of varnish if required. When completely dry thread onto nylon line.*

◀ *Make the beads a variety of shapes and colors.*

Don't leave beads to dry out completely because they will set so hard it will be difficult to pierce them.

Placing beads on cocktail sticks makes painting easier.

▲ *A heart cookie cutter makes a great template for a paper pulp pendant.*

PULP SCULPTURES

Cut out cardboard templates to use as a base for novelty designs, then sculpt layers of pulp into the shape.

PULP FICTION?

Newsprint will take longer to soften than tissue paper. Don't squeeze out too much water, or the pulp will become an unworkable mass. Excess pulp can be stored in a plastic bag and kept in the refigerator.

◀ *Use your fingers, and imagination to sculpt designs like this lip smacking brooch.*

27

Clay beads

WITH TODAY'S SYNTHETIC MODELING CLAYS, IT IS easy to make beautiful beads in unusual shapes, and different sizes. The big advantage poly clays have over air-drying clays is that they set hard at low temperatures in an oven, and won't shatter if dropped. They also come in an amazing range of colors.

Roll into spirals, and add earring backs.

MARBLE BEAD NECKLACE

Make beautiful marbled beads to create a stunning necklace. Varnish the beads to bring out the depth of the colors, then thread onto leather thong.

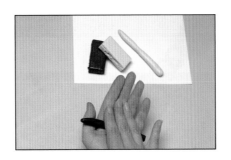

1 *Break off a piece of modeling clay, and knead until it becomes soft, and pliable. Then roll into a sausage in the palms of your hands. Do the same with each of the colors — wash your hands carefully when changing between colors.*

2 *Wrap the colored sausages around each other, as shown. Then twist them, and start to knead the different colors together, rolling the sausages carefully in the palms of your hands until they combine to form another sausage.*

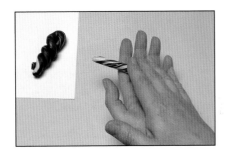

3 *Fold the sausage in half, twist the two halves together, and knead again. Roll into another sausage, and repeat the process until all the air bubbles have gone, and you have a marbled effect. Don't knead too much, or the colors will merge completely.*

4 *Place the sausage on the work surface, and cut off small pieces. Roll these in the palms of you hands to make ball or tube shaped beads. Make as many beads as you need to make a necklace, rolling out more pieces of clay if required.*

5 *Make a central hole in each bead using a knitting needle. Smooth any rough edges, and reshape by rolling in the palms of your hands. Bake in a low temperature oven following the instructions on page 34. When ready, thread onto a thong.*

▶ *This necklace and earring set is made from lots of different bead shapes, decorated with tiny blobs of other colors.*

Tie a knot either side of each bead.

Insert the metal wire before baking.

BEAUTIFUL BEADS

Have fun molding clay into a variety of shapes to make unusual beads.

◀*Roll modeling clay into thin sausages, and link both ends to make a small circle. When baked, varnish, and use to space out larger beads.*

◀*Roll out long worms of clay, and wrap them around a knitting needle to make unusual beads. Dust them with modeling clay bronze powder before baking, to make them sparkle.*

◀*Make chunky beads, and transform into a stylish bracelet to go with the spiral earrings.*

Sculptured clay jewelry

YOU CAN HAVE GREAT FUN SCULPTING CLAY into different shapes. Building up a design on a flat base — like these sheep, ladybugs, bees, and flowers — is the easiest way to start. Include loops, or holes, so the finished design can be hung as a pendant, or drop earrings. Leave an area flat for brooches, badges, hair slides, and stud earrings.

Pigs make great earrings.

WHAT YOU NEED

White modeling clay
Black modeling clay
A pair of earring findings
Strong, clear-drying
multi-purpose adhesive
Stick pin with flat disc top

SHEEP PIECES

These fun sheep earrings, and stickpin are much easier to make than they look. Once you've mastered the basics, try making other animals, too.

I Break off a piece of white clay, and knead with your fingers until it becomes soft, and pliable. Then roll into a sausage, approximately 0.5 inch in diameter. Slice off the uneven end, then cut two slices, each measuring 0.25 inch wide.

3 From black clay, mold four ears, and two triangle faces. Soften the points of the triangle with the tip of you finger, and press into place. Press the ears in position. Make three tiny white balls for each earring, and use for eyes and nose.

BAKING CLAY!

Set your oven to 110°C/200°F/Gas Mark 3, and place the clay on a cookie sheet. Bake until completely dry. This may take between five and eight hours, depending on the size and thickness of the clay. Ask an adult to help, as even low temperatures can burn if you don't take care.

2 Break off a small amount of black modeling clay, and mold two tiny balls for each earring. Press firmly to one edge of each white circle to make the feet.

▲ *Glue earring findings onto the back of sculpted ladybugs to make cute earrings.*

▲ *Mold features from tiny bits of modeling clay. Don't forget to wash your hands when changing between colors.*

CLAY CAPERS

Almost any shape can be recreated in modeling clay. Once you get used to using it you could try making cars, buses, fruit, and even miniature people.

Position one point of the triangle between the two feet.

◀ *Make the stickpin in the same way as the earrings, but use a slightly larger base.*

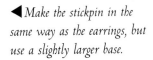

▲ *A caterpillar creeping across a leaf shape makes an amusing brooch.*

▼ *Knead the clay until it is really soft, break off small balls, and mold into petal shapes using your thumb. Pinch the ends and press together to make a fun flower brooch.*

A jewel stone glued to the center after baking gives the perfect finishing touch.

▲ *Loop long sausages into flower shapes, add a center made from a flattened ball, and brush with gold modeling clay powder, before baking, for a dazzling earring and pendant set.*

◀ *Bake in a low temperature oven, following the instructions on the left. When the sheep are cool to the touch, glue the earring findings (or stick pin) in place, and leave to set.*

Quick and easy clay shapes

Modeling clay can be rolled out just like pastry, cut into all kinds of shapes – using templates or cookie cutters – and then made into stunning jewelry. The shapes can be left as they are or, before baking, press a small jewel stone into the clay to make an indentation where you the stone to go. Remove the jewel, bake, and then replace.

WHAT YOU NEED

2 blocks of different modeling clay in contrasting colors
Rolling pin
Hair slide base (from craft stores)
Tweezers
Strong, clear-drying multi-purpose adhesive

▲ *The shapes were put onto eye pins, and painted with glitter powder before baking. The sections were joined, and the jewel stones added afterward.*

FLOWERY HAIR SLIDE

Roll out the clay, and add a flower in a contrasting color for a pretty hair slide. Rolling the clay on a foil-covered board helps stop the clay sticking.

1 *Break off some modeling clay, and knead until it becomes soft and pliable. Roll out a strip approximately 0.25 inch thick, and a little larger than the hair slide base.*

2 *Smooth out any indentations, caused by wrinkles in the foil, with your fingers. Check that the strips is the right size, and curve the ends to neaten.*

3 *Roll balls in the contrast color. Mold into petal shapes, and pinch the ends between your thumb and forefinger. Press the petals in a flower shape on the base.*

4 *Flatten a ball of the base color, and press over the center point. Press the completed design over the hair slide, and bake, following the instructions on page 34.*

▶ *Baking the design over the clip will make it curve. It is unlikely to stay in place, and will need gluing to secure.*

◀ *Cut shapes out of brightly colored clays, and place them on top of each other for fun geometric jewelry.*

SPECIAL SHAPES

Use different colored clays together to make striking designs, or decorate plain colors with special glittery powders, and ceramic paints.

▲ *A metal wire was inserted before baking the sections of these earrings. They were eased out after cooking, and a bead was placed in the center, then the wire was reinserted through the bead, and looped over an ear hook at the top, and a wired bead at the bottom.*

▶ *Modeling clay glitter powder, mixed with varnish, has been painted over these cookie cutter earrings after baking to give them a special finish.*

▼ *Brush a blob of clay with glitter powder, and bake on a ring finding.*

Glue the ring finding, and jewel stone in place after baking.

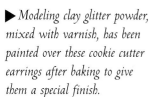

▼ *Cookie cutters were used to shape these stars. The stars were then covered with yellow ceramic paint to make them look like china. The earring findings were glued in place before painting to help hold the shape.*

Decorative effects

PRESSED COTTON BALLS ARE CHEAP TO BUY, AND make A great base for experimenting with different paint techniques. You will soon discover that different sorts of paints can give very different finishes, and that different materials can be mixed to create stunning effects. The ideas discussed on these pages can also be used to decorate plain wooden beads, and polystyrene balls.

Wooden beads have been decorated with acrylic paints, and varnished.

COTTON BALL NECKLACE

Pressed cotton balls are usually used in simple toy making, but they make great beads, too. Decorate with paint, and add detail with marker pens for a really original necklace.

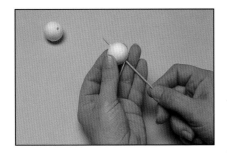

1 Use a knitting needle to pierce holes through the center of the cotton balls. (Cotton balls are frequently used as heads in toy making, and usually have a hole that goes part way through.)

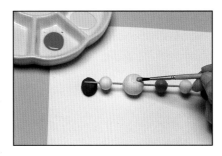

2 Thread the beads onto the knitting needle, and rest on two lumps of Plasticine — to make it easy to turn the beads as you paint. Paint the beads in different colors, and leave to dry.

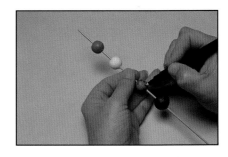

3 Draw patterns on the beads with a marker pen. Varnish the beads, to give them a harder wearing finish. Leave to dry for 24 hours before threading onto nylon line to make into a necklace.

A necklace clasp can be used to give a more professional finish.

BEAUTIFUL BEADS

Interesting paint effects give a new look to ordinary wooden beads. It's a good idea to experiment on paper first, before decorating the actual beads.

◀ *Graduate the size of the beads as you thread them on.*

▲ *Cut decorated cotton balls in half, using a craft knife (ask an adult to do this), and glue to a hair slide base.*

◀ *Link together different sized beads with jeweler's wire. Use pliers to make a loop at the bottom to stop the beads falling off, and one at the top to insert an earring hook through.*

◀ *Plain beads have been given a striking design with a fine marker pen, then mixed with bought black beads to make stylish earrings.*

▶ *Nail varnish has been used to paint these beads, and gold felt pen to draw the spots.*

Thread onto shirring elastic.

37

Dough craft

DOUGH SCULPTURE IS A traditional craft that is inexpensive and easily mastered. The dough is made from ingredients found in most kitchen cupboards – flour, salt, and water. When mixed together, they make a wonderfully versatile modeling medium that can be sculpted, rolled, or cut out, like pastry, into different shapes. Once the design is completed, the shapes are baked in an oven to harden like biscuits – but are not to be eaten! Once painted and varnished, the dough shapes make bright, fun jewelry pieces that cost next to nothing.

▲ *Bright coloured brooches make great gifts for friends or family.*

WHAT YOU NEED

Two cups of plain flour
One cup of table salt
One cup of hot water
One tablespoon of cooking oil
Mixing bowl
Tracing paper
Pencil
Card
Scissors
Rolling pin
Craft knife
Paint brushes
Felt-tip pens
Colored paints
Varnish
Brooch pin
Strong glue (epoxy)

BAKING DOUGH

Set your oven to 110°C (200°F) and place the design on a baking tray. Bake until completely dry. This may take between five and eight hours, depending on the size and thickness of the dough.

FUN FISH BROOCH

1 *Put the flour in a mixing bowl and stir in the salt. Mix in the water and oil slowly, first using a fork and then with your hand until the dough is stiff but not too sticky.*

2 *Turn the dough out onto a board and knead it for about ten minutes, until it becomes smooth. Roll out a small piece and cut out your shape, using a cardboard template if needed. Here, it is a fish shape.*

3 *Place the dough in a plastic bag or container for about an hour. Lightly moisten any add-on pieces with water and press together carefully. Bake the shape following the instructions shown above.*

COLORFUL NECKLACE AND BRACELET

Roll left-over dough into balls and pierce them with a knitting needle to make beads. Vary the shapes and sizes to add interest and paint in bright colors. String the balls onto strong nylon line to make a necklace.

Make sure the necklace fits over your head and then tie the ends.

◄ *This clay necklace is made from a number of different shapes — circles, ovals, squares, and stars. You could try making little fruit shapes — pears, apples, oranges, and bananas.*

STICKY FINGERS?

If the dough is too sticky, add a bit more flour. If it is too dry, add a little more water. Keep the dough in a bag or container until you are ready to use it. This will prevent it from drying out.

Earring fixing

◄ *These earrings match the necklace. They are made from left-over clay fastened onto an earring fixing.*

▼ *Painted clay balls have had tiny triangles of colored plastic stuck on them, to make this fun necklace.*

Triangles of colored plastic

Fabric jewelry

Y OU WOULDN'T NORMALLY THINK OF USING FABRIC to make jewelry, but if you can use a needle and thread, you can easily transform any odd scraps into stylish earrings, necklaces, and bracelets. Look out for interesting off-cuts, remnants, and even old clothes from thrift stores and yard sales. Collect sequins, and beads to use as decoration and to give a special finish.

STRAWBERRY EARRINGS

Scraps of felt and a few beads can be turned into pretty strawberry earrings to wear throughout the summer months.

WHAT YOU NEED

Tracing paper

Small piece of cardboard

Pencil

Scissors

Red felt

Tiny black rocailles

Black thread

Red thread

Small amount of wadding

Green felt

2 jump rings

Pliers

2 earring hooks

1 Trace the strawberry shape from the template, and transfer on to card. Place on the felt, and cut out 3 shapes for each earring. Sew a few black rocailles at random to each section.

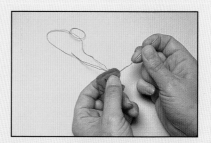

2 With wrong sides facing, backstitch the section together, leaving an opening at the top edge.

3 Pad each earring out with a little piece of wadding. Gather the top edge and secure with several stitches.

4 Cut strips of green felt. Make one edge jagged. Gather the straight edge, and stitch to the top of each strawberry. Oversew a jump ring to the top of each one. Use pliers to join the ear hook.

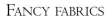

FANCY FABRICS

More unusual necklaces and bracelets are easy to make
from tubes of bright silks, filled with wadding and
twisted together. Dramatic earrings and pendants can
be made from simple shapes cut from felt and
decorated with sequins and embroidery.

▲ *If you make the tube much
longer than you need and cut
the wadding to the right length,
the fabric will form natural
gathers to give a ruched effect.*

Knot tubes together at their
centre point then stitch jump rings
and a clasp to the ends to make a
fun bracelet.

▼ *Sequins have been sewn to one side
of the fish to look like scales. Decorate
first before joining together, and
padding out with wadding. Make into
a brooch by stitching a pierced
brooch finding to the
undecorated side.*

*Leaving the tail
unstitched gives the fish a
three dimensional look.*

More fabric jewelry

Glamorous fabrics, such as velvets, net, satins, and lamés can be soaked in PVA adhesive and used to create interesting effects. Ribbons come in wonderful colors, and look great woven together and mounted on cardboard, or gathered up and turned into mini rosettes for pretty earrings. Once you start playing with fabric, you'll soon come up with your own ideas.

<table>
<tr><td>

WHAT YOU NEED

....

2 strips of ribbon,
approximately 6 in long
matching line
needle
2 earring findings with
clip-on sieve discs
Pliers
</td></tr>
</table>

ROSETTE EARRINGS

Colorful strips of ribbon gathered into rosettes make pretty earrings.

1 *Join the ribbon strips to make two circles. Work either French seams or flat seams to enclose raw edges.*

2 *Work a row of gathering stitch close to one edge and draw up tightly to form a rosette. Oversew the ends to secure.*

3 *Carefully stitch the wrong side of each rosette securely to a pierced disc.*

4 *Position the disc over a matching ear clip and bend over the clips with pliers.*

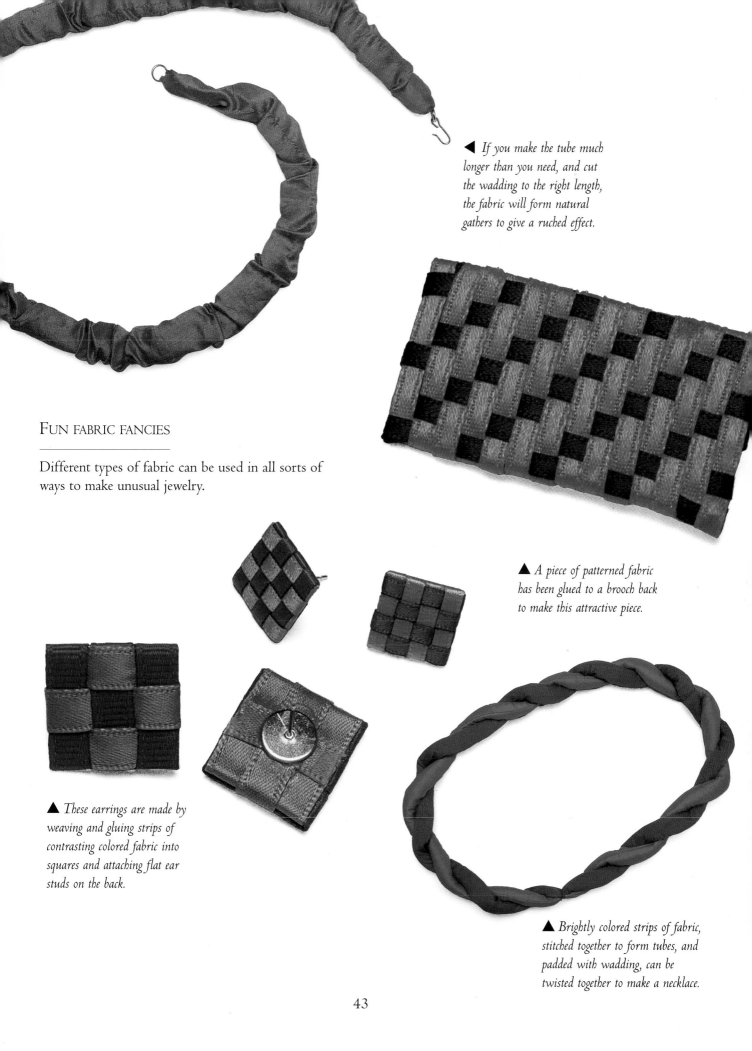

◀ *If you make the tube much longer than you need, and cut the wadding to the right length, the fabric will form natural gathers to give a ruched effect.*

FUN FABRIC FANCIES

Different types of fabric can be used in all sorts of ways to make unusual jewelry.

▲ *A piece of patterned fabric has been glued to a brooch back to make this attractive piece.*

▲ *These earrings are made by weaving and gluing strips of contrasting colored fabric into squares and attaching flat ear studs on the back.*

▲ *Brightly colored strips of fabric, stitched together to form tubes, and padded with wadding, can be twisted together to make a necklace.*

Beautiful buttons

BUTTONS CAN BE USED TO MAKE BRILLIANT PIECES OF jewelry and there are lots of different ways they can be linked and threaded together for necklaces, earrings, and bracelets which can look stylish or fun. You can also stick buttons onto hair slides, hair bands, and bracelets to give plain basics a different look. To build up a collection of buttons, take them off any old clothes you've grown out of before they get thrown away.

BLACK-AND-WHITE BRACELET

With their ready-made holes, buttons make a great substitute for beads and are easy to string together. Plain white buttons can be painted in different colors using acrylic enamel-finish paints. Alternating black and white buttons strung together on shirring elastic make a striking looking bracelet

1 Thread the needle with a double length of shirring elastic long enough to slip over your hand and sit on your wrist comfortably. Tie one end loosely to a large bead to prevent the buttons from falling off.

2 Take the needle and double thread through one hole in each button until you have threaded on enough buttons to go around your wrist. Then secure the thread with a firm knot.

BUTTON HUNT

Look out for unusual buttons at yard sales and thrift stores and ask friends and adults if they have any they don t need — many people have a button box filled with an interesting assortment.

44

▲ *Shaped buttons make great earings and all you have to do is glue an earring finding to the back.*

BUTTON BONANZA

Buttons can be used to make brilliant pieces of jewelry and there are lots of different ways they can be linked and threaded together for necklaces, earrings, and bracelets.

◀ *Buttons with loop backs (shank fastenings) look striking sewn together to make a pendant.*

▼ *This bracelet is made by stringing together a mixture of beads and buttons.*

Think about the order of beads and buttons before you start

Making your own buttons

NOW YOU'VE SEEN WHAT CAN BE DONE WITH buttons, you can have fun making your own to create unique jewelry. Use brightly colored poly clays, add decorative paint finishes to air-drying clay, or leave natural. Like beads, you can make all kinds of different shapes, and sizes, other than the traditional styles. Try making them look like candies, animals, flowers, or anything else you fancy. Then turn them into fun earrings, bracelets, or necklaces.

WHAT YOU NEED
....
A pack of terracotta air-drying clay
Rolling pin
Small cookie cutters
Knitting needle
Permanent marker pens
Nylon line
Selection of beads

FUNKY NECKLACE

Using air-drying clay, it is easy to make your own buttons shapes. Thread your buttons with beads to make a fun necklace.

1 *Roll out clay until it's about 0.25 inch thick. Use cookie cutters to make some shapes. Mold others with your hands.*

2 *Use a knitting needle to pierce holes in each shape to make them look like buttons. Leave to harden.*

3 *Decorate the edges of the hardened buttons with markers. Thread your buttons, along with beads, on to line.*

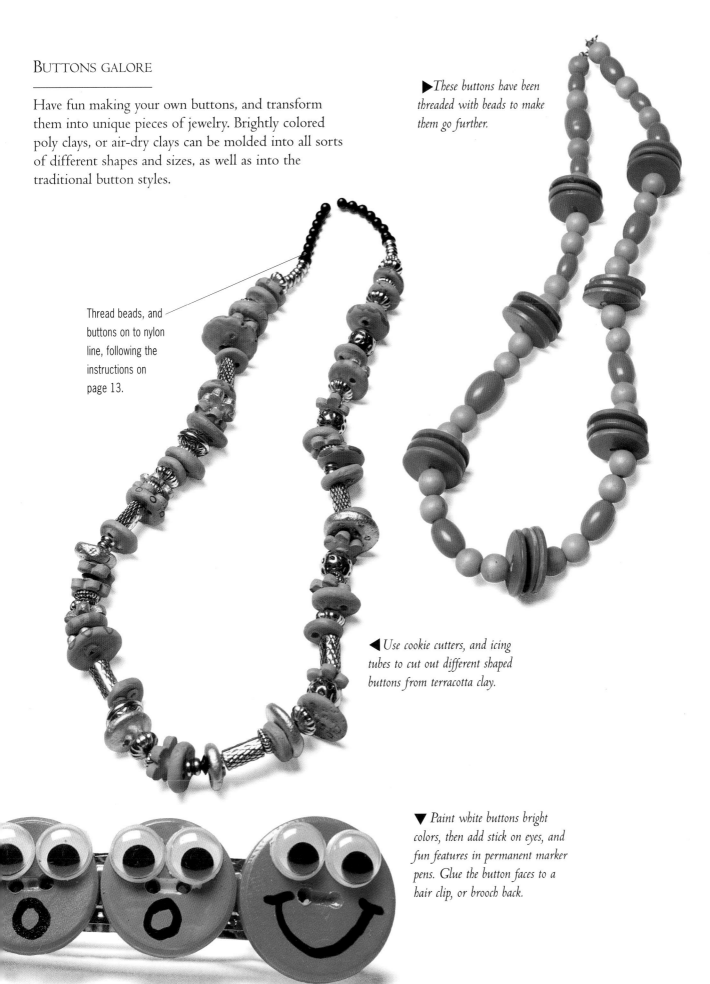

BUTTONS GALORE

Have fun making your own buttons, and transform them into unique pieces of jewelry. Brightly colored poly clays, or air-dry clays can be molded into all sorts of different shapes and sizes, as well as into the traditional button styles.

▶*These buttons have been threaded with beads to make them go further.*

Thread beads, and buttons on to nylon line, following the instructions on page 13.

◀*Use cookie cutters, and icing tubes to cut out different shaped buttons from terracotta clay.*

▼ *Paint white buttons bright colors, then add stick on eyes, and fun features in permanent marker pens. Glue the button faces to a hair clip, or brooch back.*

Fun with feathers

Y OU CAN BUY FEATHERS IN FANTASTIC COLORS from department stores, and use them to make jewelry that's glamorous and fun to wear. With findings, you can turn them into earrings, necklaces, and brooches or, alternatively, simply glue them to hair bands or slides for a really glamorous finish. Always use clean feathers, and if you find any when out walking, check with an adult before working with them.

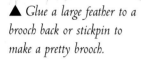

▲ *Glue a large feather to a brooch back or stickpin to make a pretty brooch.*

FEATHER EARRINGS

A brightly colored feather duster was used for these easy to make earrings. Choose co-ordinating beads to really set the feather off.

1 *Trim feathers from the duster. Lay two to three on top of each others and insert the ends through beads. Wrap wire tightly around the ends of the feathers, and make a loop to attach to the ear hook.*

2 *Use the pliers to open up the loop on the ear hook, and slip it through the loop you've made with wire on the feathers. Close the loop again securely. Neaten the feathers if necessary.*

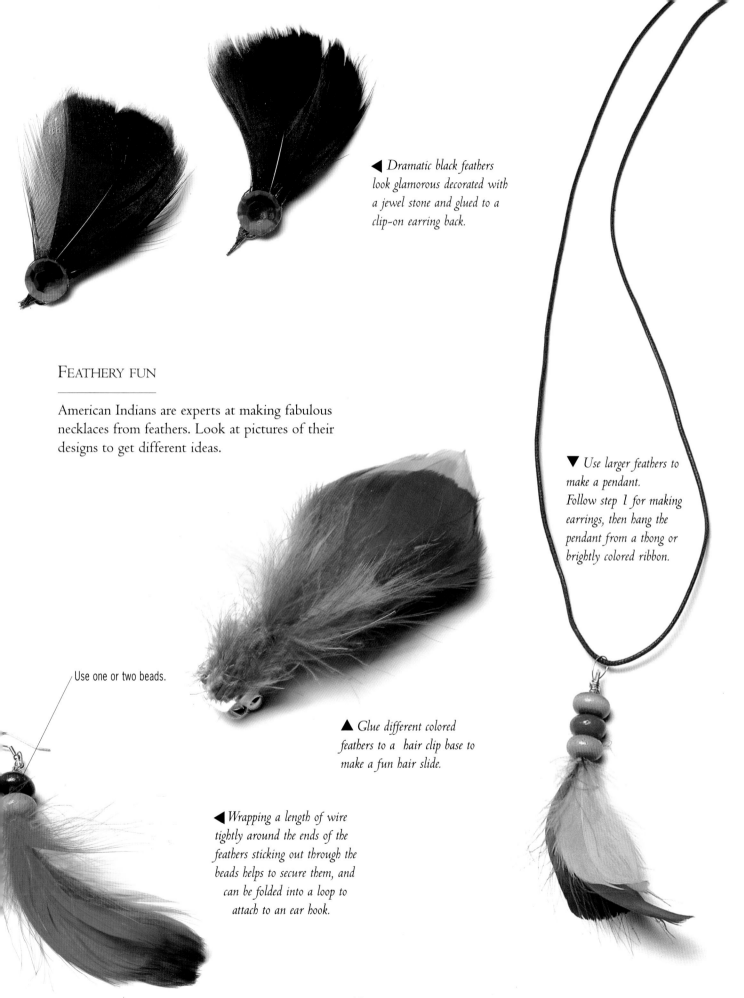

◀ *Dramatic black feathers look glamorous decorated with a jewel stone and glued to a clip-on earring back.*

FEATHERY FUN

American Indians are experts at making fabulous necklaces from feathers. Look at pictures of their designs to get different ideas.

▼ *Use larger feathers to make a pendant. Follow step 1 for making earrings, then hang the pendant from a thong or brightly colored ribbon.*

Use one or two beads.

▲ *Glue different colored feathers to a hair clip base to make a fun hair slide.*

◀ *Wrapping a length of wire tightly around the ends of the feathers sticking out through the beads helps to secure them, and can be folded into a loop to attach to an ear hook.*

Be creative with cork

Acollection of corks can be transformed into really unique jewelry. Cork is easy to work with, but you might need an adult's help with cutting, slicing, and piercing holes. Corks look great left their natural color, and simply varnished, or you can give them a bright painted finish. Thread them together on their own, or mix with home-made clay, or bought beads for different effects.

CORK NECKLACE

Slices from an ordinary wine bottle cork look great painted bright colors, and strung into necklaces alongside other beads.

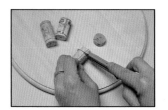

1 *Ask an adult to help you cut the cork into slices about 0.25 inch wide.*

2 *Pierce a hole through the center of each cork slice using a sharp thick needle.*

3 *Slip the cork discs on to a knitting needle. Rest this on two lumps of plasticine — this will make it easy to turn the discs as you paint. Paint the discs in different colors, and leave to dry. Varnish, if desired, and leave to dry for 24 hours before making up into jewelry.*

4 *Knot one end of a length of nylon line securely to a bolt ring clasp. Thread on a selection of beads, then start adding the cork slices, placing a bead between each disc. Finish with the same number of beads as you started with, and knot the line securely to a jump ring.*

▶ *The selection of identical beads allows the necklace to hang evenly on your neck.*

Varnish will give the cork beads a shiny finish.

◀ *Slices of unpainted cork, with just a couple of coats of varnish to bring out the grain, make stylish earring when glued to a finding.*

▶ *Self-adhesive cork has been used for this pendant. Cut it into strips, then roll-up like a paper bead, following the instructions on pages 14 and 15. Insert a wire loop into the center and secure with glue.*

CORKING IDEAS

Use different sorts of cork to create truly stunning jewelry.

▲ *Transform a champagne cork into a doll pendant. Paint on a face, and glue hair to the top of the cork. Insert an eye pin, or wire loop into the top, and thread through a length of leather thong or ribbon.*

Stylish seashells

NEXT TIME YOU ARE DOWN AT THE BEACH, LOOK out for shells to turn into exquisite necklaces, earrings, and bracelets. Some shells are soft enough for holes to be made with a big needle, but for others you will need an adult to use a bradawl or drill. Large shells can simply be threaded on to cord to make a pendant. Smaller ones can be linked together to make bracelets and earrings.

WHAT YOU NEED
....
A selection of shells
Plastic hair band
Strong clear-drying
multi-purpose adhesive

▲ *Attach jump rings to shells to make attractive drop earrings.*

SHELL HAIR BAND

Keep any small shells you collect on holiday, and use to decorate a plain hair band.

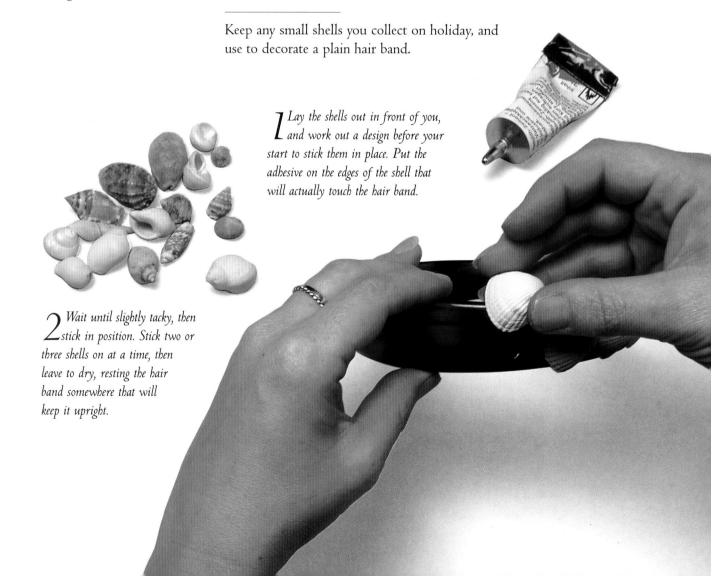

1 Lay the shells out in front of you, and work out a design before your start to stick them in place. Put the adhesive on the edges of the shell that will actually touch the hair band.

2 Wait until slightly tacky, then stick in position. Stick two or three shells on at a time, then leave to dry, resting the hair band somewhere that will keep it upright.

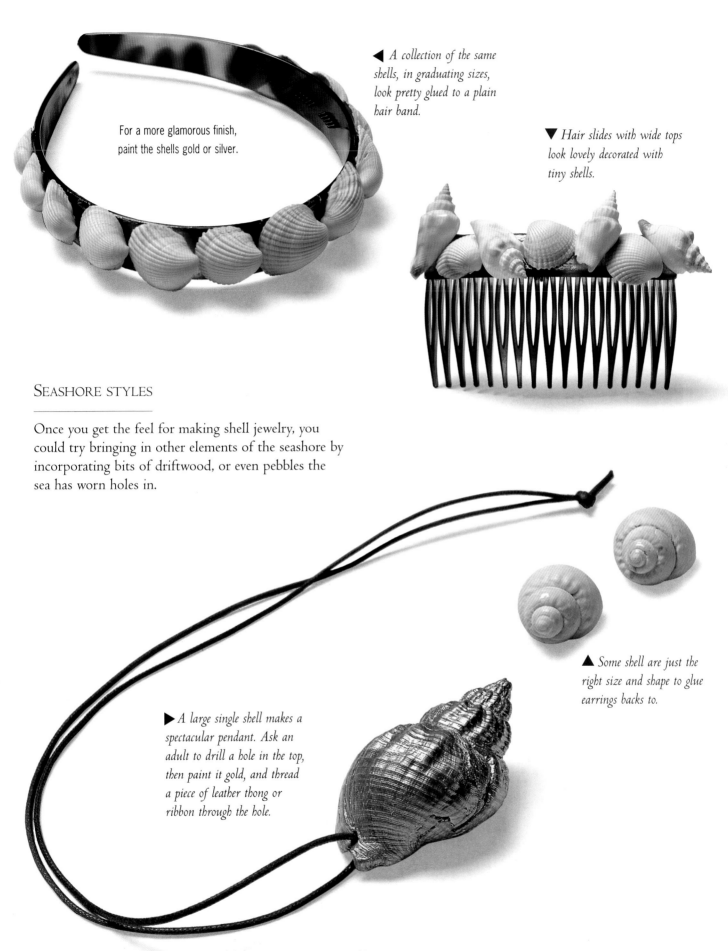

For a more glamorous finish,
paint the shells gold or silver.

◀ *A collection of the same
shells, in graduating sizes,
look pretty glued to a plain
hair band.*

▼ *Hair slides with wide tops
look lovely decorated with
tiny shells.*

SEASHORE STYLES

Once you get the feel for making shell jewelry, you
could try bringing in other elements of the seashore by
incorporating bits of driftwood, or even pebbles the
sea has worn holes in.

▲ *Some shell are just the
right size and shape to glue
earrings backs to.*

▶ *A large single shell makes a
spectacular pendant. Ask an
adult to drill a hole in the top,
then paint it gold, and thread
a piece of leather thong or
ribbon through the hole.*

Seeds and nuts

SEEDS AND NUTS ARE OTHER MATERIALS FROM nature that you can use successfully in jewelry making. Nuts, stung on to nylon, make unusual necklaces. Melon seeds, washed and dried, or sunflower seeds look wonderful strung together for necklaces, bracelets, and even earrings, but can also be used to decorate other plain bases.

PEANUT NECKLACE

I Pierce a hole through the top of each nut with a sharp thick needle.

PEANUT NECKLACE

It's easy to make holes in the shells of monkey nuts with a large tapestry needle. Paint them gold, and string together with pearl beads to make a pretty necklace.

2 Paint the nuts gold. Inserting a cocktail stick through the hole will make it easier to hold and rotate the nuts while painting.

WHAT YOU NEED

A bag of monkey nuts

A thick sharp needle

Gold paint

Paintbrush

Nylon line

Pearl beads

▲ *Make earrings to match a necklace to create a pretty set.*

3 Loosely tie the nylon line to a pearl bead to stop all the others falling off. Thread several pearl beads on, then add the peanuts, putting a pearl bead between each one. Finish the necklace with the same number of pearl beads as at the beginning. Untie the end bead, and knot the two ends together. Trim any excess nylon.

Tie on a stopper bead
before threading the seeds.

▶ *Next time you eat a melon,
keep the seeds, and make them
into a delicate necklace. Wash,
and dry them first, then use a
needle to thread them on to
nylon line*

TASTY IDEAS

Seeds and pulses look really good
painted and used to decorate basic
cardboard bases.

▲ *Decorate a circle of card
with sunflower seeds to make
an unusual brooch.*

▲ *Stick pumpkin seeds to a
cardboard base to make a flower
shape, then add earring backs.*

Pasta and pulses

Raiding the pantry can provide you with all sorts of materials to use in jewelry making. Dried pasta tubes can be painted in brilliant colors, and transformed into fun necklaces. Lentils and other pulses can be stuck to all kinds of bases – cardboard shapes, bangles, plastic hair bands, and slides. Paint with metallic paint for a glamorous finish.

▲ *A cardboard tube was cut in half lengthways, covered in lentils, and painted a dramatic black.*

▶*Pasta shapes can also make pretty earrings.*

PASTA NECKLACE

Dried pasta comes in a whole range of fun shapes, which look wonderful painted, and threaded into necklaces. Don't squeeze the pasta shapes too hard, or they will shatter, but don't worry if just a few bits break off .

1 *Push the needle gently through the pasta shapes to make a hole for the line to go through. Try not to use too much pressure.*

2 *Put the shape on top of a wooden skewer, and paint with a fine brush. Stick the skewer into a foam pad, or ball of plasticine, and leave to dry.*

3 *When dry, outline the edges in a contrasting color. Leave to dry, then varnish, if desired. Leave for 24 hours before threading into a necklace.*

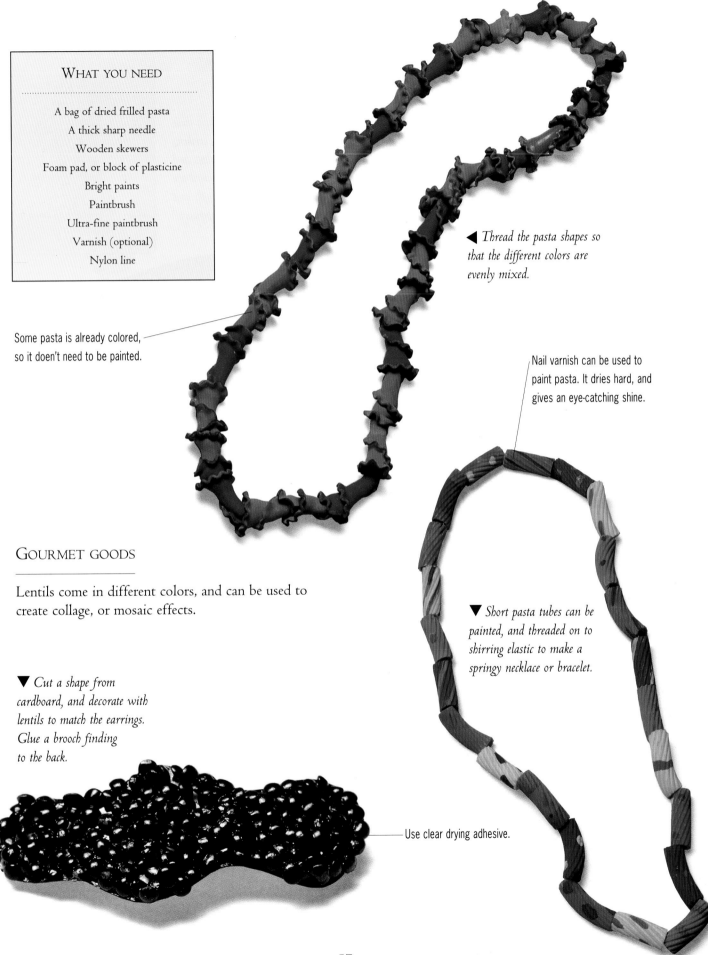

A bag of dried frilled pasta

A thick sharp needle

Wooden skewers

Foam pad, or block of plasticine

Bright paints

Paintbrush

Ultra-fine paintbrush

Varnish (optional)

Nylon line

◀ *Thread the pasta shapes so that the different colors are evenly mixed.*

Some pasta is already colored, so it doesn't need to be painted.

Nail varnish can be used to paint pasta. It dries hard, and gives an eye-catching shine.

GOURMET GOODS

Lentils come in different colors, and can be used to create collage, or mosaic effects.

▼ *Short pasta tubes can be painted, and threaded on to shirring elastic to make a springy necklace or bracelet.*

▼ *Cut a shape from cardboard, and decorate with lentils to match the earrings. Glue a brooch finding to the back.*

Use clear drying adhesive.

57

Tool box treasures

ONCE YOU GET THE JEWELRY MAKING BUG, YOU'LL start to look for all sorts of different materials to use. You'll be amazed at what you can find to use in a basic household tool box. Silvery nuts and washers can be linked together, and mixed with beads to look really glamorous. Washers can be painted with enamel paints to give them a bright fun look. Even plastic covered wire can be twisted or braided together into truly original bangles.

▲ *Stick three nuts together, and add earring backs.*

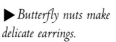
► *Butterfly nuts make delicate earrings.*

WHAT YOU NEED

....

A packet of small metal washers

Jump rings

A screw clasp

Pliers

WASHER BRACELET

Metal washers can be linked together to make a fashionable chain bracelet.

1 *Use pliers to carefully open a jump ring sideways. Slip the loop of one part of the screw clasp over the jump ring, then add a washer, and close the ring with the pliers so it's two ends meet perfectly. Open another jump ring.*

2 *Slip the jump jump ring through the first washer, then add another washer before closing. Continue linking the washers until they are long enough to fit your wrist. Add another jump ring to the last washer, and attach the screw clasp.*

▼ These tiny washers, found in a box at a yard sale, make a fun bracelet strung on to shirring elastic.

◀ Link beads, washers, and nuts together to make pretty drop earrings.

IRONWARE ITEMS

Use a little imagination, and turn ordinary bits and pieces into dazzling jewelry.

▲ Paint metal washers with enamel paints. Add gold decoration with metallic pens when dry. Glue to a hair slide base, and stick a few glass rocaille beads in the center of each washer.

▼ Hexagonal nuts can be stuck together to make brooches or pendants. Lay them out on a flat surface first, and experiment with different shapes.

◀ Larger nuts, decorated with glamorous jewel stones, make perfect earrings.

Use an adhesive suitable for metals.

61

Take a ball of string

YOU WILL BE AMAZED AT THE VARIETY OF stylish jewelry you can make with a simple ball of string. String can be braided, crocheted, and worked in macramé style to make unusual necklaces and bracelets. Glued to cardboard bases, it can be transformed into earrings and brooches. To give your string jewelry a special finish, decorate it with metallic paints or beads.

▲ *Glue a spiral of string to a large circle of cardboard to make a brooch to match the earrings opposite.*

STRING PENDANT

This pendant is really easy to make. The string is wound into a spiral around a central wooden bead, then hung from a length of leather thong

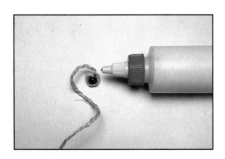

1 *Take the length of string and dab a small blob of adhesive on one end. Insert this end through the hole in the bead. Hold until it sets, then leave to dry. When dry, start winding the string around itself in a flat spiral.*

2 *As you wind the spiral, add blobs of adhesive along the string's length. Work one or two rounds at a time, then leave the adhesive to set. Keep the string in place while it dries with a peg. Continue until the spiral is almost the size you want.*

3 *At the start of the last round make a loop. Glue the loop, then leave to dry with a peg holding it in position. Finish the last round, adding a blob of adhesive to secure. When dry, thread the thong through the string loop, and knot the ends.*

STRIKING STRING SUNDRIES

Just look around at all the different thicknesses and colors of string available and you'll find lots of inspiration for unique designs of your own. A book on knots is also a good source of ideas.

Braiding is a simple way to make a string necklace. This one has been decorated with beads and simple tassels. To make the tassels, fold a length of string in half. Push the looped end through the braid from the wrong side, and then insert the end through the loop, and pull up quite tightly.

▶*Wind string around a wooden or plastic bangle, gluing as you go along. Finish by decorating with metallic paint.*

Stipple with gold paint to add a more decorative finish.

ather thong

Ensure that the loop is secure.

Use a bright colored bead.

▲ *Cut small circles of cardboard, and use glue a long length of string to each one in a spiral effect.*

Clever ideas for curtain rings

WOODEN CURTAINS RINGS ARE EASY TO TRANSFORM into items of jewelry, such as hoop earrings, or pendant necklaces. They usually have a ready-made brass loop screwed into the top that makes it simple to attach to thong, cord, or ear hooks. Brass curtain rings can quickly be turned into hoop earrings, and make really stylish bracelets when linked together with jump rings.

Brass curtain rings make pretty chain bracelets.

CURTAIN RING EARRINGS

Ricrac braid is zigzag-shaped material often used as a trimming on clothing. You can use it in jewelry to give a new look to curtain rings, transforming them into attractive drop earrings.

WHAT YOU NEED

2 wooden curtain rings

Ricrac braid

Acrylic paint in colors that co-ordinate with the braid

Paintbrush

Strong, clear-drying multi-purpose adhesive

Jewel stone

Jump rings

Pliers

Ear hooks

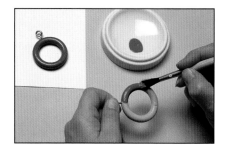

1 Paint the curtain rings, so that they are covered completely. This may take at least two coats.

2 Glue end of braid to ring. Wrap braid over ring, gluing it in place where it touches the ring. When covered, glue the end.

3 Open up a jump ring using pliers, and slip through the brass loop on the curtain ring, and the loop on the earring hook. Close so its ends meet perfectly.

▶ *Paint wooden curtain rings in white with black dots, and join earring wires to the loops at the top.*

RADICAL RINGS

Curtains rings can be painted, wrapped with braid, dressed up with glittery jewel stones, or simply linked together to make totally original jewelry.

▲ *Ricrac braid comes in a wide range of different colors, so experiment with different combinations.*

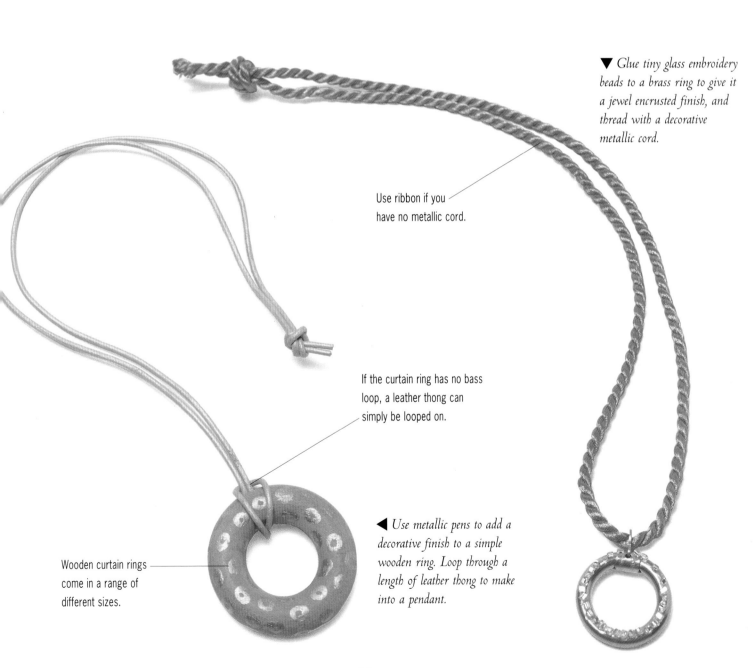

▼ *Glue tiny glass embroidery beads to a brass ring to give it a jewel encrusted finish, and thread with a decorative metallic cord.*

Use ribbon if you have no metallic cord.

If the curtain ring has no bass loop, a leather thong can simply be looped on.

◀ *Use metallic pens to add a decorative finish to a simple wooden ring. Loop through a length of leather thong to make into a pendant.*

Wooden curtain rings come in a range of different sizes.

Brightening up basic bangles

BASIC PLASTIC OR WOODEN BANGLES CAN BE GIVEN A new lease of life with a little creative thought. One of the easiest ways is to cover them with decorative cord, raffia, fabric, or even colored ribbon. Glittering, flat-backed jewel stones can be used to add a touch of glitz, and glamor, or you can simply paint them with brilliantly colored acrylic paints.

Cord is easy to wrap over bangles.

BRILLIANT BANGLES

Wrapping a plain plastic or wooden bangle with jazzy cord, or decorating with brilliant jewel stones, turns something ordinary into something really special.

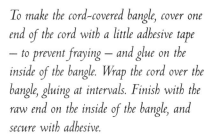

To make the cord-covered bangle, cover one end of the cord with a little adhesive tape — to prevent fraying — and glue on the inside of the bangle. Wrap the cord over the bangle, gluing at intervals. Finish with the raw end on the inside of the bangle, and secure with adhesive.

WHAT YOU NEED

A plain plastic or wooden bangle
Strong, clear-drying multi-purpose adhesive
A piece of cord, long enough to wrap over the bangle to cover completely, or a selection of flat-backed jewel stones

1 *To make the jewel-encrusted bangle, measure the circumference of the bangle, and decide how many stones you want to use. (It's also a good idea to plan how you're going to mix the colors.) Put a small blob of adhesive on the side of the bangle, and leave until slightly tacky.*

2 *Place the first flat-backed jewel stone on the glue, and hold in position until firmly set. Repeat with the remaining jewel stones, until the whole circumference of the bangle is covered — you can place the jewel stones side-by-side, or leave a regular gap between each one.*

BUSY BANGLES

Fabric soaked in PVA adhesive can be used to achieve interesting effects. When it dries, it becomes hard and rigid, and can be scrunched, pleated, or molded into many different shapes.

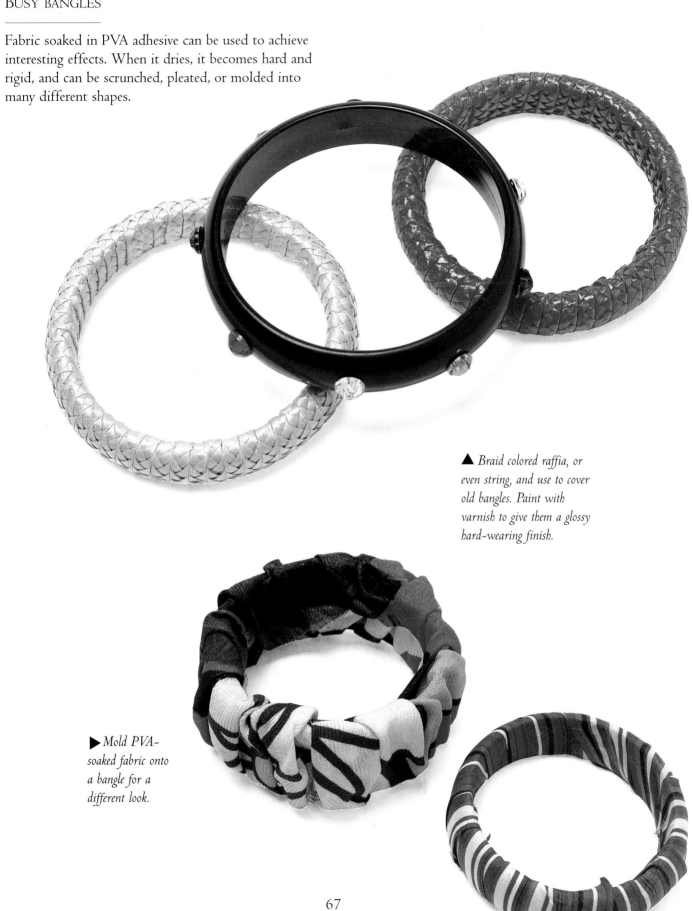

▲ *Braid colored raffia, or even string, and use to cover old bangles. Paint with varnish to give them a glossy hard-wearing finish.*

▶ *Mold PVA-soaked fabric onto a bangle for a different look.*

Professional techniques

Throughout this book we have shown you how to make pieces of jewelry from regular materials. Here we show you how to make professional looking necklaces and bracelets from bought beads and "findings." Manipulating the tiny findings may look difficult, but with a little patience you'll soon master the techniques described here.

Place a small spacer between each bead.

WHAT YOU NEED

(For Strung Necklace)
Nylon line
2 calotte crimps
2 jump rings
A bolt ring clasp
A selection of colored beads
Small gold beads
Round-nosed pliers
Snipe-nosed pliers

(For Linked Bead Necklace)
Eye pins, head pins, or jeweler's wire
Jump rings
Round-nosed pliers
A second pair of pliers
A selection of beads
Bolt ring clasp

(For Multi-strand Bracelet)
A three-stranded jewelry clasp
6 small looped calottes
Nylon line
A selection of colored beads
Small silver beads
Round-nosed pliers
Snipe-nosed pliers

SIMPLE STRUNG NECKLACE

Decide how long you want your necklace to be, then select a line.

USING CALOTTE CRIMPS

Calotte crimps are useful for concealing knots. Use pliers to open up the two sides of the calotte crimp. Make a large knot in the line, and place in the center on one side of the calotte. Close the other side over it with pliers.

1 *Cut the line to the length required, plus a little extra for knotting. Secure with a calotte crimp (see tip box). Open up a jump ring (See page 72), and slip though the loop on the calotte crimp and the loop on the bolt ring clasp.*

2 *Close the jump ring by twisting the two ends together until they meet perfectly. Thread the beads until you reach the required length. Knot the line close to the last bead, and conceal with a calotte crimp. Join to a jump ring.*

LINKED BEAD NECKLACE

Beads can be linked using wire instead of line. Eye pins are the easiest to use as they have a pre-formed loop, but you can use head pins or jeweler's wire. Headpins are like blunt pins, and you will need to snip off their "head" before making two loops with pliers. Simply loop jeweler's wire.

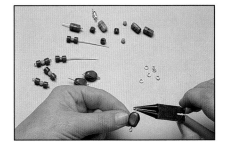

1 *Wire the beads singularly, or in groups, by inserting an eye pin, head pin, or jeweler's wire through the hole(s). Trim, and use round-nosed pliers to make a loop in the opposite end.*

2 *. Carefully open up a jump ring, and slip through the loops on each bead, or group of beads. Close the jump ring by twisting the two ends together so that they meet perfectly.*

▶ *Link the beads until you have the length required. Join a jump ring to one end, and to a bolt ring clasp. Join a jump ring to the other side, and to the second part of the clasp.*

Large beads can be wired separately, and smaller ones in groups.

1 *Attach each line to a calotte, as described on page 70. Undo its loop, and attach to the holes in the clasp using pliers. Thread on as many colored beads as required, placing a silver spacer bead between each one.*

MULTI-STRAND BRACELET

As for all projects, work out the length of the finished bracelet before starting. For this multi-strand bracelet, you will need to cut three lengths of line. Looped calottes are useful when working with a multi-strand clasp. They open from the top, whereas regular calotte crimps open from the side. To use, push the nylon line through the hole in the bottom of the looped calotte, and make a large knot. Close the calotte over the knot, and carefully secure using pliers.

◀ *Finish the lines by inserting each one through a looped calotte. Knot the line, and close the calotte with pliers. Join the calotte loops to the clasp as before.*

71

Exquisite earrings

EARRINGS ARE SOME OF THE EASIEST PIECES of jewelry to make, and there are hundreds of styles to choose from. There are lots of other ideas shown throughout the book, but here we show the simplest ways to make professional looking earrings.

STUD EARRINGS

These are the simplest earrings to make, and can be put together in minutes. Leave the adhesive to set before wearing them.

I *If working with light bases, the ear stud can be glued to the center of the wrong side. For heavier ornaments, it is important to glue nearer to the top to prevent it falling forward when being worn.*

2 *Apply adhesive to both the base, and the ear stud, and leave until tacky before sticking together. Leave for 24 hours before wearing.*

OPENING AND CLOSING JUMP RINGS

It is tempting to just pull jump rings apart to open them, but this distorts the shape, and makes them difficult to close again. The best way to do it is to hold the ring with two pairs of pliers, and twist the ends sideways, away from each other. To close, just twist back together again until the ends meet perfectly.

WHAT YOU NEED

A pair of flat ear studs and butterfly fastenings

Flat-backed jewel stones, buttons, or pieces of shell

Strong, clear-drying multi-purpose adhesive

SIMPLE DROP EARRINGS

Glass beads come in all shapes and sizes, but these tubes are perfect for making pretty dangles.

WHAT YOU NEED

4 tube-shaped glass beads

4 head pins

Wire cutters

Round-nosed pliers, to form loops

A second pair of pliers, to assist with opening and closing jump rings

2 Ear Hooks

1 Slip each bead on to a head pin. If the head begins to slip though the beads, thread on a small glass rocaille bead first. Trim the head pin to the correct length, leaving enough to make loop. Turn a loop using round-nosed pliers.

2 Carefully open up a jump ring, and slip though the loops at the top of two beads. Close the jump ring so that its two ends meet perfectly. Open up the loop at the bottom of an ear hook, and close over the jump ring.

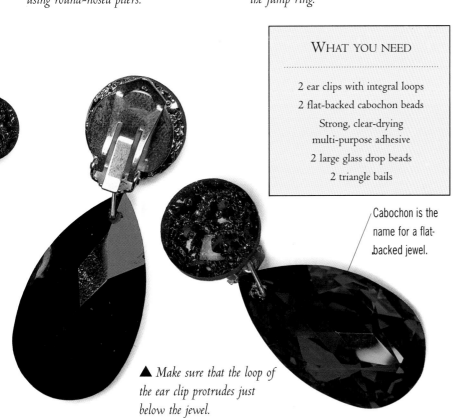

▲ *Make sure that the loop of the ear clip protrudes just below the jewel.*

WHAT YOU NEED

2 ear clips with integral loops

2 flat-backed cabochon beads

Strong, clear-drying multi-purpose adhesive

2 large glass drop beads

2 triangle bails

Cabochon is the name for a flat-backed jewel.

CABOCHAN DROP EARRINGS

These glamorous earrings take no time at all to make.

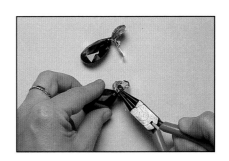

1 Glue the cabochons to the ear clips. Leave to dry. Using pliers, open up the triangle bail, and slip it through the loop of the ear clip, and then through each side of the drop bead. Use pliers the squeeze gently together to secure.

Terrific tassels

A TASSEL CAN BE USED TO ADD THE PERFECT finishing touch to a necklace, worn as a stylish pendant on it's own, or made into pretty earrings. You can make them from beads, or thread, in designs as simple, or as elaborate as you choose. Thread tassels are the simplest, and are made by wrapping long lengths over a piece of cardboard.

▲ *Wrap lengths of embroidery thread over a piece of cardboard, the length you want the finished tassel to be. Thread a tapestry needle, and slip under one looped end of the threads on the cardboard, and tie tightly. Slip the threads off the cardboard, and wrap a contrasting thread tightly near the top. Snip the other end with scissors, and fluff out the tassel. Join an earring wire to the top thread.*

BEADED TASSEL NECKLACE

Beaded tassels add an elegant finishing touch to a necklace.

WHAT YOU NEED
....
Strong nylon line
(for the necklace)
Fine invisible line
(for the beaded strands)
Fine beading needle
Medium needle
Small clear plastic beads
A large contrasting bead
A calotte crimp
Pliers

MAKING A BEADED TASSEL NECKLACE

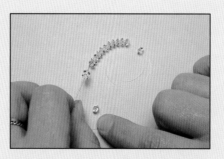 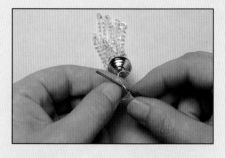

1 *Decide on the number and length of strands you want to make the tassel. Thread the beading needle with line, and string on the beads. Take the needle back through all the beads, except the last one — this prevents the others falling off.*

2 *Take both tails of each beaded strand through the large bead. When all the strands are through the bead, knot them securely close to the bead — make a loose knot, insert a needle in its center, and use it to push it up close to the bead.*

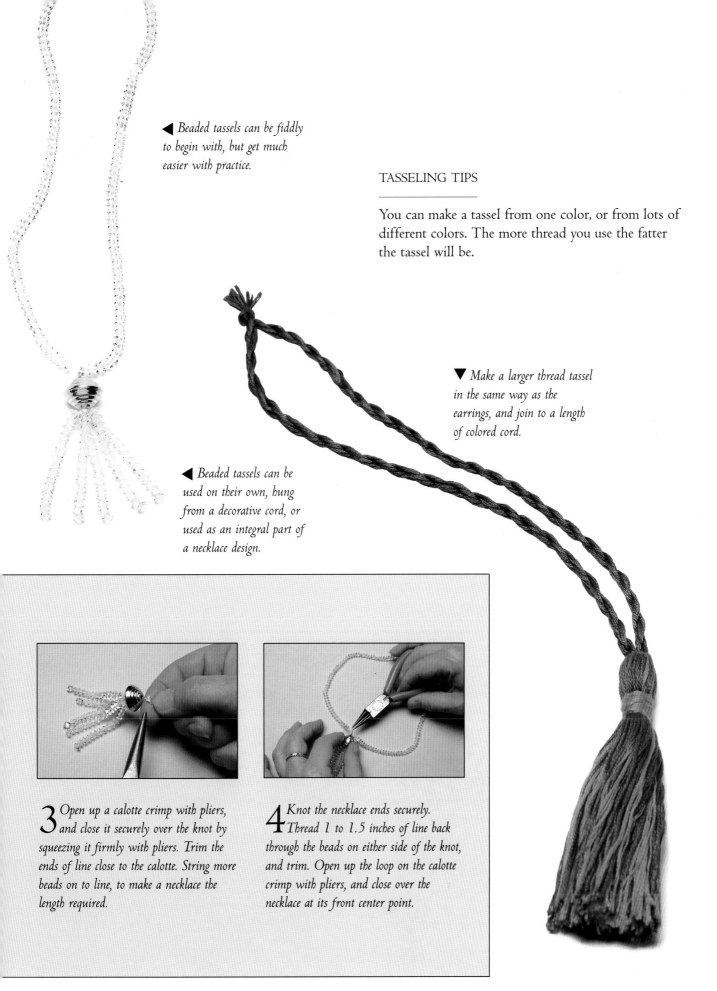

◀ *Beaded tassels can be fiddly
to begin with, but get much
easier with practice.*

TASSELING TIPS

You can make a tassel from one color, or from lots of
different colors. The more thread you use the fatter
the tassel will be.

▼ *Make a larger thread tassel
in the same way as the
earrings, and join to a length
of colored cord.*

◀ *Beaded tassels can be
used on their own, hung
from a decorative cord, or
used as an integral part of
a necklace design.*

3 *Open up a calotte crimp with pliers,
and close it securely over the knot by
squeezing it firmly with pliers. Trim the
ends of line close to the calotte. String more
beads on to line, to make a necklace the
length required.*

4 *Knot the necklace ends securely.
Thread 1 to 1.5 inches of line back
through the beads on either side of the knot,
and trim. Open up the loop on the calotte
crimp with pliers, and close over the
necklace at its front center point.*

Wrapped with style

ONE WAY TO DISPLAY A BEAUTIFUL OBJECT THAT doesn't have a pre-drilled hole is to wrap it decoratively with wire. This simple technique, provides lots of scope for experimenting with different effects. Jeweler's wire is available in gold and silver, and in a variety of thicknesses. The finest is the easiest to work with, but more interesting finishes can be achieved with the thicker ones, which need pliers and a little practice to bend and shape.

SPIRAL EARRINGS

Wrap fine jeweler's wire around a pair of snipe-nosed pliers to make a loose coil, and link to a glittering crystal bead to make a dazzling pair of earrings.

<table>
<tr><td colspan="2" align="center">WHAT YOU NEED</td></tr>
<tr><td colspan="2" align="center">Fine silver colored jeweler's wire</td></tr>
<tr><td colspan="2" align="center">Craft scissors</td></tr>
<tr><td colspan="2" align="center">Snipe-nosed pliers, to wrap the wire over</td></tr>
<tr><td colspan="2" align="center">Round-nosed pliers, to make the loops</td></tr>
<tr><td colspan="2" align="center">Two drop beads</td></tr>
<tr><td colspan="2" align="center">2 Ear hooks</td></tr>
</table>

MAKING SPIRAL EARRINGS

1 *Make a loop in one end of a length of wire. Grip this between the jaws of the pliers at the widest end. Wrap the wire tightly along the length. Trim any excess wire with scissors.*

2 *Using pliers, open the loop on the ear hook, and slip over the loop on the wire spiral you have just made. Close securely with pliers. Repeat the whole process for the other earring.*

3 *Slip the other end of the wire spiral through the hole of a drop bead, and make a loop with pliers to secure it in position. You can stretch the earring spiral, to make it looser if you wish.*

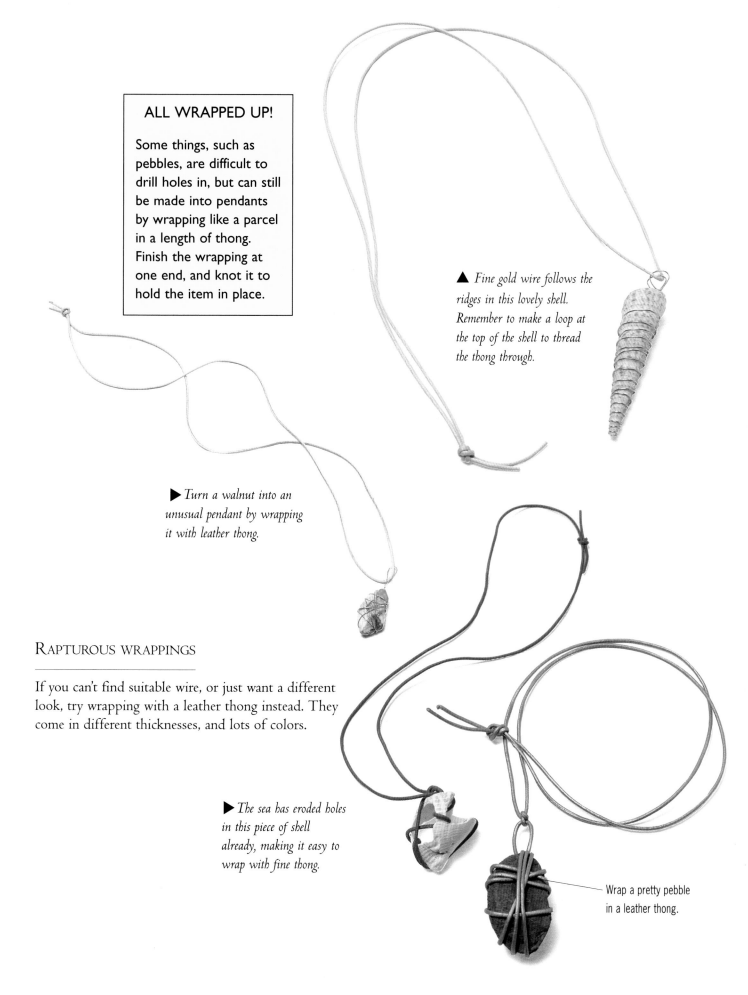

▲ *Fine gold wire follows the ridges in this lovely shell. Remember to make a loop at the top of the shell to thread the thong through.*

▶ *Turn a walnut into an unusual pendant by wrapping it with leather thong.*

RAPTUROUS WRAPPINGS

If you can't find suitable wire, or just want a different look, try wrapping with a leather thong instead. They come in different thicknesses, and lots of colors.

▶ *The sea has eroded holes in this piece of shell already, making it easy to wrap with fine thong.*

Wrap a pretty pebble in a leather thong.

77

Sensational safety pins

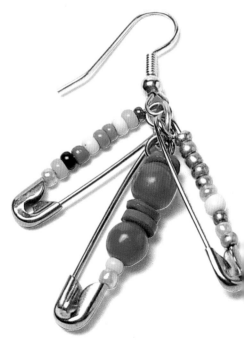

SAFETY PIN JEWELRY WAS MADE FAMOUS MOST recently by punk rockers back in the seventies. Decorated with small glass rocailles, bugle beads, or other small beads, it is easy to disguise their appearance, and make absolutely stunning jewelry. You can get all kinds of different effects by varying the beads, and mixing assorted sizes of pins together.

WHAT YOU NEED

25 to 30 gold colored safety pins of the same size

A selection of rocailles, bugle beads, and other small beads, to decorate the pins

Pliers

Small beads, to thread between the pins

Needle

Shirring elastic

A large stopper bead

SAFETY PIN BRACELET

Decorated with small beads, the safety pins are almost unrecognisable as the base for this bracelet.

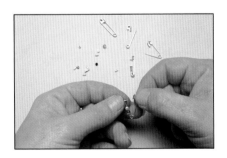

1 *Open up a safety pin, and thread on a random selection of rocailles, bugle beads, and other small beads. Close the pin, and squeeze the head with pliers to make sure it stays closed. Decorate the rest of the safety pins in the same way. Thread the needle with elastic, long enough to fit your wrist comfortably when stretched, plus a little extra. Tie the loose end to a large bead to stop the pins falling off.*

2 *Thread the pins on to the shirring elastic, with the beaded edges facing the same way, and alternating them — take the needle through the head of one pin, through a few small beads, and then through the base hole of the next pin. Continue until all the pins have been strung. Knot the ends together securely. Work the bottom thread in the same way, adding the same number of beads between each pin.*

▼ *Thread different sized beads on to safety pin, and join several together to make fun earrings.*

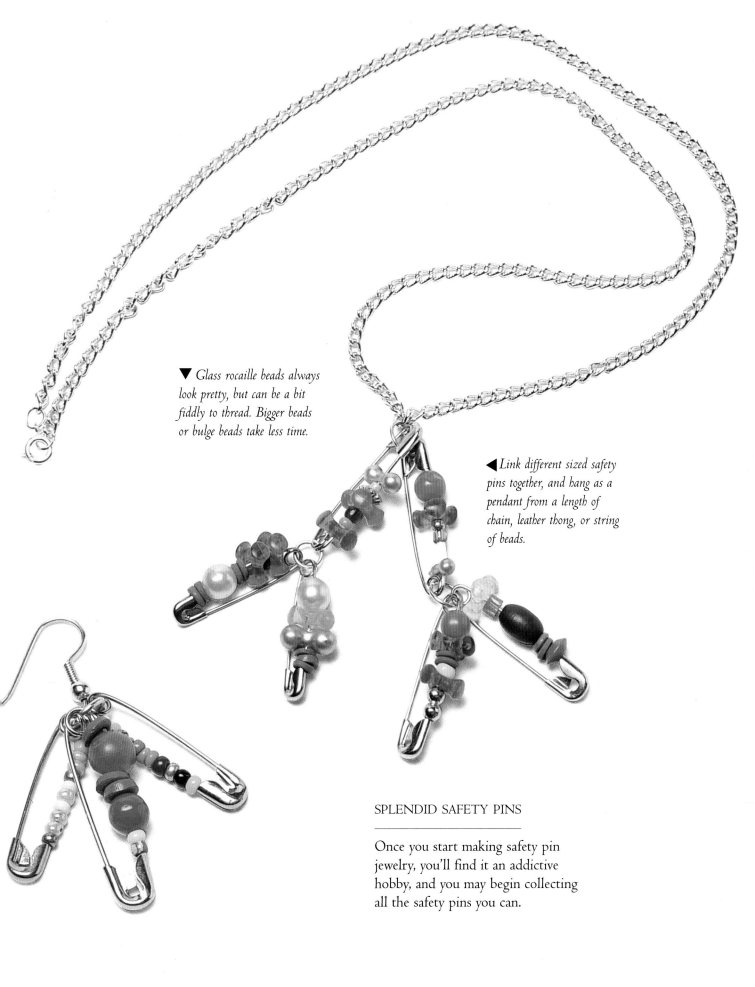

▼ *Glass rocaille beads always look pretty, but can be a bit fiddly to thread. Bigger beads or bulge beads take less time.*

◀ *Link different sized safety pins together, and hang as a pendant from a length of chain, leather thong, or string of beads.*

SPLENDID SAFETY PINS

Once you start making safety pin jewelry, you'll find it an addictive hobby, and you may begin collecting all the safety pins you can.

Magnificent millefiori

G LASS MILLEFIORI, OR "A THOUSAND FLOWER" beads, were made by people living in Venice, Italy, several hundred years ago, and were much sought after all over the world. Today, a similar effect can be achieved with simple modeling clay. Different colors are rolled, and wrapped around each other to make the "millefiori cane," which is cut into slices, and used to cover a base bead. The cane can also be used on its own to make eye-catching jewelry.

WHAT YOU NEED

Modeling clay in four
different colors,
for the cane

A selection of different
colored modeling clay, for
the base beads

Rolling pin

Round-bladed kitchen knife

Knitting needle

Varnish (optional)

MILLEFIORI BEADS

Create beautiful millefiori-style beads from different colored modeling clay. Spraying with paint or varnish will bring out the lovely colors, but leave for 24 hours before making into jewelry.

GETTING STARTED

Knead the modeling clay with your thumbs and fingers, until really soft and pliable. Wash your hand when changing colors – to prevent one rubbing off on the other, and spoiling the finished effect.

MAKING BEADS

1 Roll out two sheets of colored clay to a depth of about 0.1 inch. Place one on top of the other, and press gently together, smoothing out any air pockets. Roll together like a Swiss roll, smooth the edge, gently compress, and roll between the palms of your hands.

2 Roll out four sausages of equal lengths from each of the remaining colors, to a diameter of 0.5 inches. Build the cane by alternating these sausages around the two color spiral, as shown. Gently compress together, and roll between the palms of your hands.

3 Roll out another sheet of modeling clay, choosing one of the colors used for the spiral, and use to wrap around the outside of cane. Smooth the joining edge, gently compress together, so that there are no air pockets, and roll between the palms of your hand.

◄ *Bake slices on a hair slide base, so they curve to fit. Glue in place when cool.*

SIMPLE SLICES

Slices from a thick millefiori cane can be used on their own to make colorful jewelry. Follow the basic instructions, but don't roll out the cane as thinly.

▶ *Cut slices that graduate in size, and use a cocktail stick to pierce holes, from side to side, instead of through the center. After baking, string together on nylon line to make a colorful necklace.*

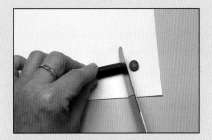

4 Roll the cane carefully, and evenly on a flat surface with the tips of your fingers, until the diameter is about 0.25 inch. The diameter of the cane should be roughly the same throughout its width. Try to ensure that no air pockets build up.

5 Cut off the end of the cane. Discard this first bit, as it will be misshapen, then cut the rest of the cane into thin slices. Put these aside, and gently roll the clay into balls, or tubes between the palms of your hands, to make the base beads.

6 Cover each bead with the millefiori slices, and roll gently to merge them together. Leave for several hours before piercing a hole in each with a knitting needle. Bake in a low temperature oven, following the instructions on page 34. (Ask an adult to supervise this stage.)

Colorful threads

Y OU CAN MAKE BRILLIANTLY COLORED
FRIENDSHIP bracelets, hair ties, and unusual
necklaces by knotting, braiding, and weaving
cotton embroidery threads together. Mix
different colors together to get striking
combinations, and add your own personal
touch by stitching co-ordinating or
contrasting beads to the finished design.

Experiment with different
numbers of threads and
a mix of colors

GETTING STARTED

Cut two 30-inch-long strands from each skein of cotton
and knot them together 5 inches in from one end. Stick
the safety pin through the knot and secure to the
pincushion. Hold the pincushion between your knees as
you work. Separate the strands, so that the two on the
outside are the same color, the next colors in toward the
center are the same, and the two middle ones are the
same.

FRIENDSHIP BRACELET

Make your own friendship
bracelets from brilliantly colored
cotton embroidery threads.

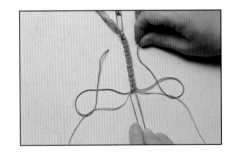

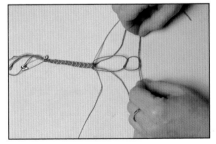

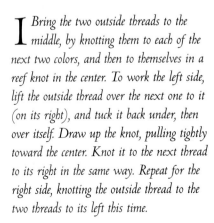

1 *Bring the two outside threads to the
middle, by knotting them to each of the
next two colors, and then to themselves in a
reef knot in the center. To work the left side,
lift the outside thread over the next one to it
(on its right), and tuck it back under, then
over itself. Draw up the knot, pulling tightly
toward the center. Knot it to the next thread
to its right in the same way. Repeat for the
right side, knotting the outside thread to the
two threads to its left this time.*

2 *When the two outside threads have
reached the middle, knot them to
themselves by taking the left over the right,
and under, then the right over the left, and
under. This completes one row. Continue to
work as many rows as you need to make a
strip long enough to fit comfortably around
your wrist, taking the outside threads to the
center each time in the same way, and
always working with the same color thread
on both sides.*

FANCY THREADS

Braid, knot, and weave bright threads together to make bracelets, hair ties, and unusual necklaces.

Thread on beads at regular intervals as you work.

▼ Split the threads, and add beads to one section, and continue to weave the rest, then bring the two together again to make a more interesting necklace.

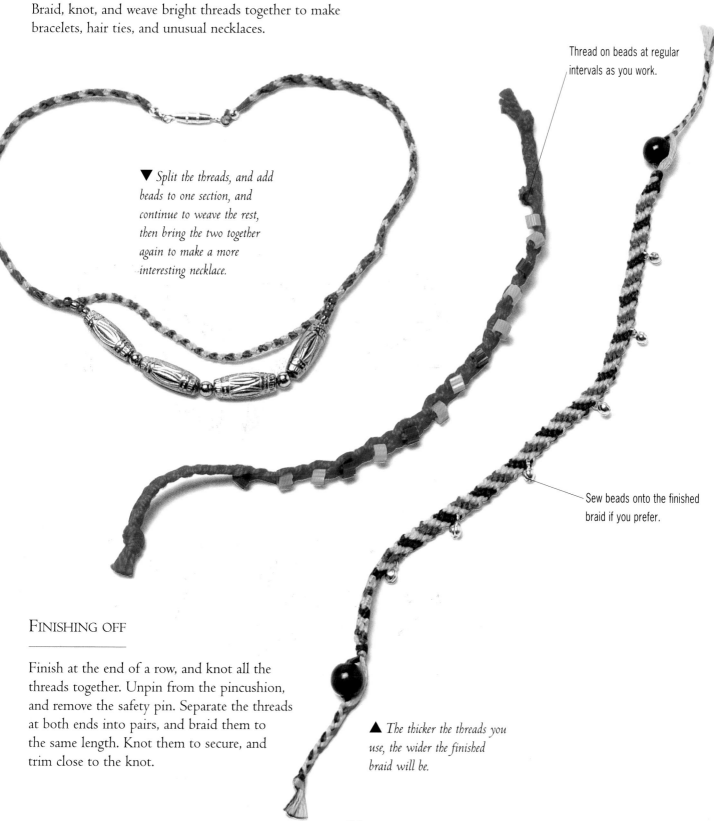

Sew beads onto the finished braid if you prefer.

FINISHING OFF

Finish at the end of a row, and knot all the threads together. Unpin from the pincushion, and remove the safety pin. Separate the threads at both ends into pairs, and braid them to the same length. Knot them to secure, and trim close to the knot.

▲ The thicker the threads you use, the wider the finished braid will be.

Loom weaving

METAL OR WOODEN LOOMS ARE EASY TO FIND IN craft stores and can be used to create all kind of wonderful jewelry designs. Look for inspiration from colorful native American and African beadwork. Looms are simple to thread and can be used to make elaborate designs not only with beads, but cotton line too. Weaving with thread is very rewarding but takes a lot of time and concentration and you won't be able to use the loom for anything else until you've completed the piece.

BEADED PENDANT

Roughly work out a design on a piece of graph paper first; here, we are making a colorful pendant. Once the loom is threaded, it is much easier to work the designs than it looks.

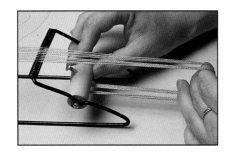

1 Thread the loom with one more "warp" (lengthways) line than you need for the pattern. Add 5 inches to the finished length of your project or the loom (whichever is bigger). Cut the lines and knot together at one end.

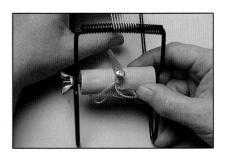

2 Separate into two halves and loop over the screw in one roller. Turn the roller until you can knot and place the lines over the screw in the other roller. Turn this until the lines are taut and separate each line into its own slot on the separator bar.

WHAT YOU NEED

A small beading loom
Colored silk embroidery line
Fine polyester or silk beading line
A fine beading needle
Selection of beads
Screw clasp
Pliers

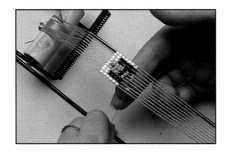

3 Work out how much beading line you need by multiplying the number of rows in the design by its width, then adding an extra 12 inches. Knot the thread neatly to an outside warp thread leaving a 3-inch tail.

4 Thread the needle and pick up a row of beads, bring them up under the warp threads and push them up between each warp thread. Take the needle back through the beads making sure it is above the warp threads. Add beads in rows.

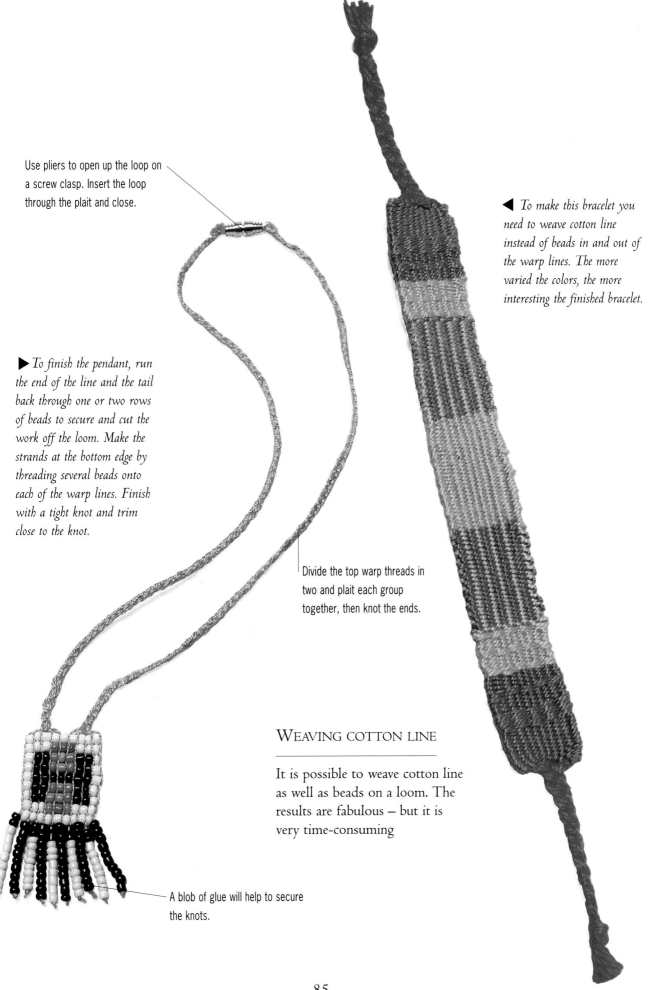

Use pliers to open up the loop on a screw clasp. Insert the loop through the plait and close.

◀ *To make this bracelet you need to weave cotton line instead of beads in and out of the warp lines. The more varied the colors, the more interesting the finished bracelet.*

▶ *To finish the pendant, run the end of the line and the tail back through one or two rows of beads to secure and cut the work off the loom. Make the strands at the bottom edge by threading several beads onto each of the warp lines. Finish with a tight knot and trim close to the knot.*

Divide the top warp threads in two and plait each group together, then knot the ends.

WEAVING COTTON LINE

It is possible to weave cotton line as well as beads on a loom. The results are fabulous – but it is very time-consuming

A blob of glue will help to secure the knots.

Easter holidays jewelry

COLORFUL BROOCHES, EARRINGS, AND HAIR SLIDES ADD a touch of fun to Easter holiday outfits, and make great presents, too. Use the simple ideas shown here to inspire your own designs. Clay or cardboard can be cut, shaped, and decorated in endless ways, and the craft foam used to make the bunny hair slide is very versatile.

BIRD'S NEST SET

A fun bird's nest, complete with colorful eggs, has been made into a brooch and earring set that will brighten up the holiday.

WHAT YOU NEED

Brown modeling clay

Small amounts of colored modeling clay, for the eggs

Brooch back

Earring findings

Strong clear-drying multi-purpose adhesive

1 Roll out balls of brown modeling clay, and squash flat with your thumb to make the bases — make the base for the brooch bigger than those for the earrings. Roll more brown clay into tiny sausage shapes of different lengths, and use to build up a nest shape on the base.

3 Wash your hands to remove any traces of brown modeling clay, and then mold small egg shapes in different colors. Position these inside the nest, pressing gently in place. Bake in a low temperature oven, following the instructions on page 34. (Ask an adult to supervise this stage.)

2 When the nest is the right size, add a few more shorter "sticks" to the middle, for the eggs to sit on.

4 Glue a brooch back to the base of the larger nest, and earring findings to the smaller nests.

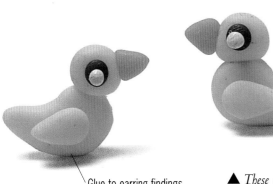

Glue to earring findings.

▲ *These ducks are easy to make from modeling clay. Cut out wing shapes, and features separately, then press in place before baking.*

EASTER EXTRAS

Think of all the things you like best about Easter, and turn them into fun pieces of jewelry. Spring flowers, Easter bonnets, and Easter bunnies are just a few ideas.

TRICKY CLAY!

If you find rolling out tiny clay sausages (such as those used for the nests) fiddly, try pushing the clay through a garlic press after it has been kneaded until soft and pliable.

◀ *Easter egg paper, rescued from the trash, was used to make these stylish beads, using the method shown on page 28.*

◀ *Craft foam comes in wonderful colors, and can be cut just like cardboard or felt. Draw out your design, cut round it, and glue to a hair slide base. Add detail with a permanent marker pen.*

Happy halloween

Make some ghoulish jewelry to wear when trick or treating, or to a special Halloween party. Spiders are always creepy, and really easy to sculpt in modeling clay, and turn into spooky earrings, or brooches. Bright orange clay in perfect for pumpkins – make them look ghoulish by adding spooky features. Make a large pumpkin for a brooch, and two smaller ones for matching earrings.

SPIDER SET

Spooky spiders are perfect for trick or treating. These earrings are made out of modeling clay, and can be finished with an earring hook, or clip-on back. The spider pendant is wonderfully simple to make using a pressed cotton ball, pipe cleaners, and stick on eyes – all available from craft stores.

1 *Break off a small piece of black modeling clay, and knead with your fingers until soft. Roll two balls, and squash each flat with your thumb to make the earring bases.*

2 *Roll out tiny black sausages. Lay across the base, curving the ends downward to make legs. Make two for each earring, making the bottom one shorter than the top one. Press firmly in place.*

3 *Wash your hands, then roll two tiny balls from the white clay. Squash flat, and press in position for the eyes, on the opposite side to the legs. Add black pupils, and a tiny red strip for the mouth.*

4 *Insert the eye pin through the top of the spider before baking. Harden in a low temperature oven, following the instructions on page 34. Leave to cool, then attach earring hooks.*

5 *To make the spider pendant, paint the cotton ball black, and glue eyes in place. Insert pipe cleaners as legs, and glue to secure. Insert the eye pin, and glue. Loop through a length of leather thong.*

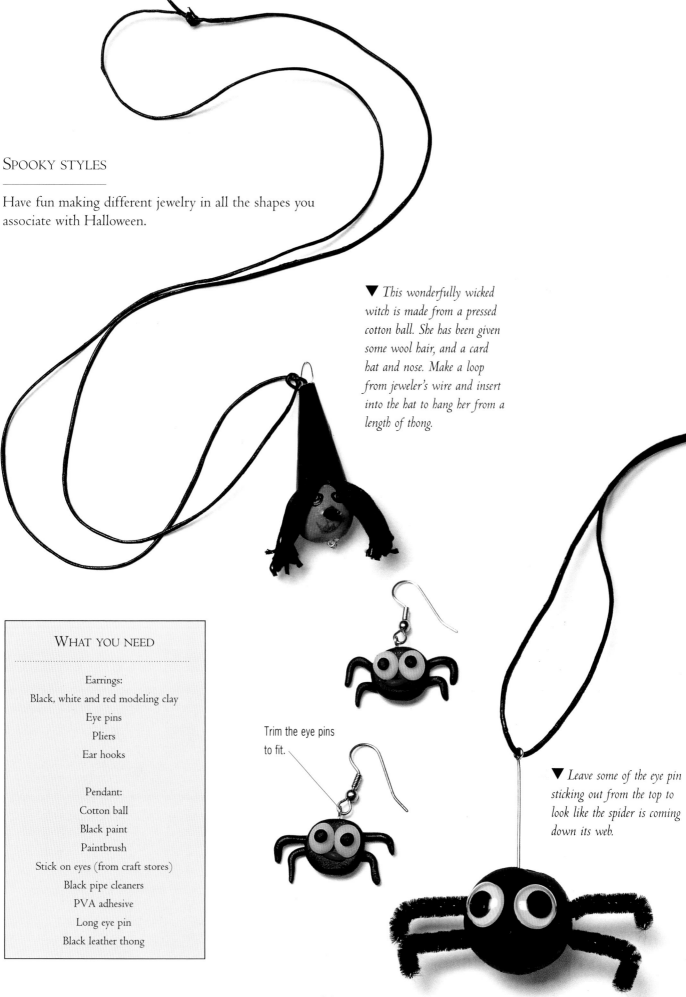

SPOOKY STYLES

Have fun making different jewelry in all the shapes you
associate with Halloween.

▼ *This wonderfully wicked
witch is made from a pressed
cotton ball. She has been given
some wool hair, and a card
hat and nose. Make a loop
from jeweler's wire and insert
into the hat to hang her from a
length of thong.*

WHAT YOU NEED

Earrings:

Black, white and red modeling clay

Eye pins

Pliers

Ear hooks

Pendant:

Cotton ball

Black paint

Paintbrush

Stick on eyes (from craft stores)

Black pipe cleaners

PVA adhesive

Long eye pin

Black leather thong

Trim the eye pins
to fit.

▼ *Leave some of the eye pin
sticking out from the top to
look like the spider is coming
down its web.*

89

Festive fun

CHRISTMAS IS A TIME FOR DRESSING UP, AND YOU CAN add the perfect finishing touch to a favorite outfit by making your own festive jewelry. Modeling clay is easy to mold into shapes that can then be decorated. Give it a glittery finish by brushing on a special powder before baking, or simply mix a little varnish with glitter.

Mold a jolly snowman.

CHRISTMAS TREE EARRINGS

Glittering Christmas tree earrings add the perfect finishing touch to a festive outfit.

WHAT YOU NEED

Green modeling clay
Brown modeling clay
Round-bladed kitchen knife
Modeling clay glitter powder
Paintbrush
2 eye pins
Pliers
2 Jump rings
2 Ear hooks

CHRISTMAS TREE EARRINGS

1 *Break off a small piece of green modeling clay, and knead with your fingers until soft. Roll out into a sausage that tapers. Starting from the point of the sausage, cut off five discs, each about 0.1 inch in depth.*

2 *Place the discs on top of each other, and press gently together. Break off a tiny ball of green clay, and add to the top of the tree. Break off a small ball of the brown clay, and mold to make the trunk. Press into place.*

3 *Brush with glitter powder, and insert an eye pin, trimmed to fit, through each tree top. Bake in a low temperature oven, following the instructions on page 34. (Ask an adult to supervise this stage.)*

4 *Use pliers to open up the jump rings, and push through the eye pins on each baked tree. Close the rings. Open up the loops on the ear hooks, and slip through the jump rings. Close the loops again securely.*

MORE IDEAS

Enjoy making your own fun jewelry to wear throughout the festive season, or to give to family, and friends as presents.

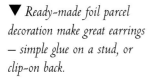

▼ *Ready-made foil parcel decoration make great earrings — simple glue on a stud, or clip-on back.*

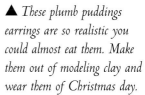

▲ *These plumb puddings earrings are so realistic you could almost eat them. Make them out of modeling clay and wear them of Christmas day.*

▼ *Decorate a plain hair comb with festive tinsel. Wrap around the top bar, taking the tinsel in, and out of the comb's teeth.*

▼ *These festive earrings would make an ideal Christmas present.*

Index

Page numbers in *italic* refer
to illustrations or captions
on those pages.